Earl Thollander's
Back Roads of California

Store and Post Office,
Plumas County

Books by Earl Thollander BACK ROADS OF WASHINGTON
BACK ROADS OF OREGON
BACK ROADS OF CALIFORNIA
SCENIC BYWAYS OF ARIZONA
BACK ROADS OF THE CAROLINAS
BACK ROADS OF TEXAS
BACK ROADS OF NEW ENGLAND
EARL THOLLANDER'S SAN
FRANCISCO

BARNS OF CALIFORNIA

ASAHI BEER
BOOSER BIER
WARNING: PEPPOP
HEALTH SAYS BOOSER
IS HARMLESS IF
LEFT IN THE BOTTLE

COKE

A. RUBES TOOLS

OREDAZAC ORACLE
~NOTHING~
ABSOLUTELY NOTHING
EVER HAPPENED HERE UNTIL THE YEAR 1871.
A. RUBE LOST HIS WAGONLOAD OF SUPPLIES
THAT HE WAS BRINGING FROM PETALUMA WHEN
HE ATTEMPTED TO FORD AUSTIN CREEK AT THIS SPOT-
FLOUR, BEER, COFFEE, BACON, BEANS, POWDER, JEANS
AND TOOLS ALL HAD TO BE AGAIN BROUGHT FROM
PORT PETALUMA TO SUPPLY HIS FAMILY NEEDS.

NOTHING, ABSOLUTELY NOTHING ELSE HAPPENED
HERE UNTIL THE YEAR OF ECOLOGY
1971 WHEN THIS MEMORIAL WAS ERECTED
AS THE LAST RESTING PLACE OF THESE
BOTTLES OF
NO~RETURN

Folk art sketched near Cazadero (Oredazac spelled backward), Sonoma County

Earl Thollander's
Back Roads of California

65 Trips on California's Scenic Byways

UPDATED EDITION

SASQUATCH BOOKS
SEATTLE

*to dear friends
Bill and Barbara*

Second printing 1994.

Printed in the United States of America.

Originally published in 1983 by Clarkson N. Potter, Inc.

Cover illustration and calligraphy by Earl Thollander.

Library of Congress Cataloging in Publication Data
Thollander, Earl.
     [Back roads of California]
     Earl Thollander's back roads of California: 65 trips on
California's scenic byways.—Updated ed.
        p.   cm.
     Includes index.
     ISBN 1-57061-009-6: $12.95
     1. California—Guidebooks. 2. Automobile travel—
California—Guidebooks. I. Title.
F859.3.T525   1994   94-5738
917.9404'53—dc20   CIP

Sasquatch Books
1008 Western Avenue
Seattle, Washington 98104
(206) 467-4300

Bush
Penstemon,
Santa Clara County

Contents

Rural mailbox,
Knoxville Road, Napa County

5

Central California

Map legend

. ___5.6___ . distance in miles between dots

→ → → my route (which may be reversed should you desire)

▲ campgrounds
■ towns and cities
▭ dams
– – – lake boundaries
–.–.– trails
.... rivers
▢ special place
✕ my sketching place
⌂ church
⊓ picnic grounds
⊡ cemetery
△ mountains
⌂ buildings

NORTH is always toward the top of the page

Southern California

napa county

I am grateful to the artist Joe Seney for his good companionship on many of these back road journeys.

Turkey Buzzard,
Stanislaus County

Preface

It has been over a decade since I compiled this nonhighway travel guide to California's out-of-the-way places, and more than 20 years since its companion volume, Back Roads of California, appeared. During that time, much has changed, but thankfully, much has remained the same. The back roads and scenic byways described here are as beautiful as when I first explored them. They offer a different way of experiencing our often too-hectic world—a more contemplative pace, quieter landscapes, and the discovery of nearly forgotten treasures.

Each of the book's four parts begins with a sectional map. These will help you locate the back roads on larger maps that are available from many sources, including travel services, chambers of commerce, gas stations, tourist bureaus, and automobile clubs. Localized maps for all roads throughout the book will guide you on specific trips. Arrows trace my direction of travel, although the routes can easily be reversed. The North Pole is toward the top of the page. Maps are not to scale because the roads are of varying lengths; however, the mileage notations will provide a sense of their distance.

Your odometer will not measure distance exactly the same as mine, but the differences should not be too great. AAA county and regional maps were essential to me in following the back roads. I also purchased maps at ranger stations when entering forest preserves. All maps and text have been carefully checked for this updated edition.

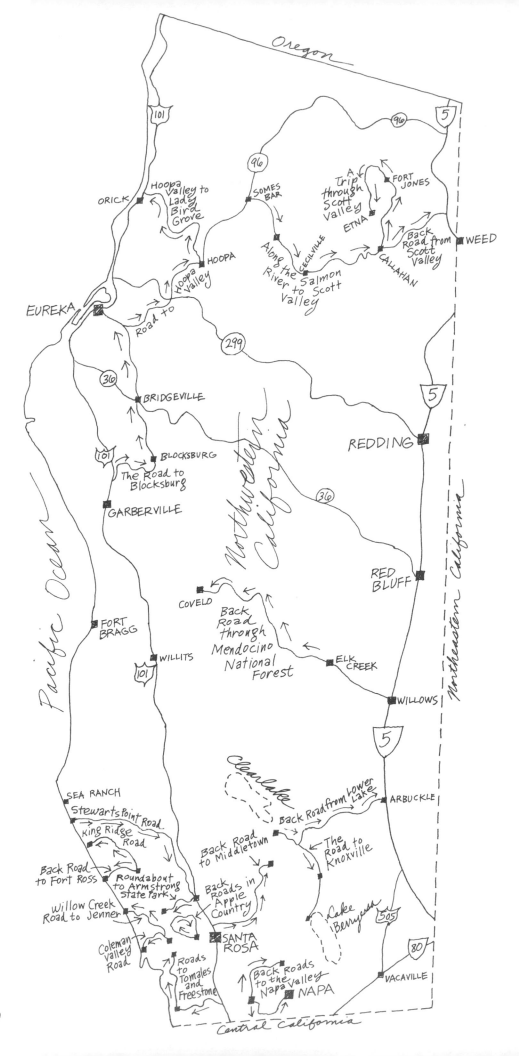

Oregon

101

96

ORICK
Hoopa Valley to Lady Bird Grove

SOMES BAR

A Trip through Scott Valley
FORT JONES
ETNA
CECILVILLE

HOOPA
Hoopa Valley

Back Road from Scott Valley
CALLAHAN

WEED

Along the Salmon River to Scott Valley

EUREKA
Road to

299

36

BRIDGEVILLE

REDDING

5

101
BLOCKSBURG
The Road to Blocksburg

GARBERVILLE

Northwestern California

36

RED BLUFF

COVELO
Back Road through Mendocino National Forest

FORT BRAGG

WILLITS
101

ELK CREEK

WILLOWS

Northeastern California

5

Clearlake

SEA RANCH
Stewarts Point Road
King Ridge Road

Back Road from Lower Lake
ARBUCKLE

Back Road to Fort Ross
Roundabout to Armstrong State Park

Back Road to Middletown

The Road to Knoxville

Willow Creek Road to Jenner

Back Roads in Apple Country

Lake Berryessa

505

Coleman Valley Road

SANTA ROSA

80

Roads to Tomales and Freestone

Back Roads to the Napa Valley
NAPA

VACAVILLE

Central California

Pacific Ocean

I've heard people boast of how fast they went somewhere and how many miles were covered in the time. In the pages that follow there are mountain and coastal roads to enjoy with no regard for speed or the hour.

I start early and let the day unfold. I don't push to get anywhere because I know that the fun and beauty of the back road experience is in the trip itself.

I hesitate to divulge certain roads, but it would be unrealistic to believe they can be saved from change by hiding them. Only for a while, perhaps. And, of course, they are not secret. They are public roads and are catalogued on county maps.

Better to announce their charm and beauty and alert everyone interested to guard against infringements upon them. I also like to think that back road travelers like myself will not drop trash or create disturbances along the way.

Those who live on the back roads and we who enjoy traveling them must be concerned that they remain unspoiled as long as possible.

California Poppy, Tehama County

Roads to Tomales and Freestone

Rolling pastureland, cows, old farms, leaning barns, and rows of eucalyptus distinguish this area of California. I sketch along Carmody Road with a meadowlark's song in the still morning air.
Curious cows peer at me, then go back to munching the green grass.
The village of Tomales was established at the head of Keyes Creek with the opening of a store there in 1852. Tomales made its first rail shipment of produce to Sausalito — via the North Pacific Coast Railroad — in 1874, when 300 sacks of potatoes were delivered to be ferried across the Golden Gate to San Francisco.

The view from Carmody Road, Marin and Sonoma counties

14

I sketch the town from across the hills, then drive to nearby Dillon Beach overlooking Bodega Bay. The bay was named by its discoverer, Juan Francisco de la Bodega y Cuadro, in 1775.

The village of Tomales, Marin County

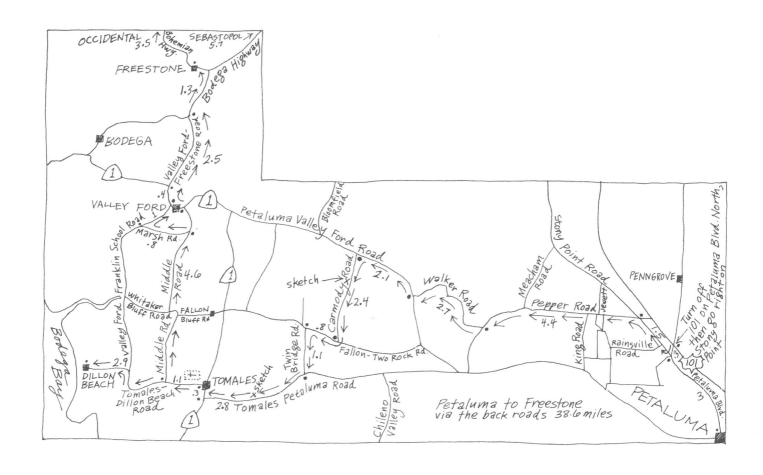

Map labels:

OCCIDENTAL 3.5 ↑ Bohemian Hwy. / SEBASTOPOL 5.7 ↗
FREESTONE
Bodega Highway
1.3 ↑
BODEGA
1
Valley Ford-Freestone Road
2.5
Valley Ford
.4
VALLEY FORD
1
Marsh Rd. .8
Petaluma Valley Ford Road
Bloomfield Road
Franklin School Road
Whitaker Bluff Road
Valley Ford
Middle Road 4.6
FALLON
Fallon Bluff Rd.
sketch
Carmody Road
2.1
2.4
Walker Road
2.7
Meacham Road
Stony Point Road
PENNGROVE
Turn off 101 on Petaluma Blvd. North, then go right on Stony Point
Pepper Road
4.4
Jewett
1.5
Bodega Bay
Middle Road
Twin Bridge Rd.
.8
Fallon-Two Rock Rd.
1.1
King Road
Rainsville Road
101
Dillon Beach 2.9
DILLON BEACH
1.1
TOMALES
.3
sketch
2.8 Tomales Petaluma Road
Tomales-Dillon Beach Road
1
Chileno Valley Road
Petaluma to Freestone via the back roads 38.6 miles
PETALUMA
Petaluma Blvd.
3

Back roads bring me to Freestone. The town derived its name from a kind of easily worked, or free, sandstone quarry nearby. I sketch the old, restored hilltop schoolhouse. The original railroad hostelry, known as Hinds Hotel in 1873, is still there, today called Freestone House. I also investigate the interesting plant nursery and zoo.

Old schoolhouse at Freestone, Sonoma County

Coleman Valley Road to the sea

I begin a journey to the coast on Coleman Valley Road off Occidental town's Third Street. The road winds through hilly meadow and forest. Trees are less in evidence as I approach the coast and sheep roam the smooth green hillsides. The road becomes a ridge route with views all around. Fields of low-growing purple iris are in bloom in the spring landscape. Deep green ravines and rows of coastal mountains carry the eye further and further until the sea comes into view. On the ridge above the ocean I sketch the old Irish Hill Ranch, originally owned by the Fitzgeralds. I hear that the ranch owners switched from cows to sheep farming during the Second World War because the lights required for early milkings were banned by wartime coastal blackout controls. It was easier to raise sheep than to lightproof a big, old barn or milk a whole herd of cows in the dark.

From Irish Hill to the sea

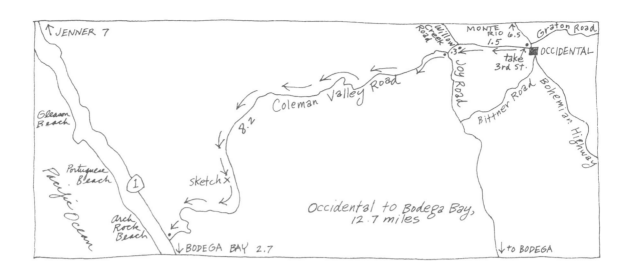

↑ JENNER 7

Gleason Beach

Pacific Ocean

Portuguese Beach

①

Arch Rock Beach

sketch X

8.2

Coleman Valley Road

Willow Creek Road

MONTE RIO 6.5 ↑

.3

Joy Road

take 3rd St.

Graton Road

■ OCCIDENTAL

Bittner Road

Bohemian Highway

Occidental to Bodega Bay, 12.7 miles

↓ BODEGA BAY 2.7

↓ to BODEGA

Willow Creek Road to Jenner

From the end of Occidental's hilly Third Street, I sketch the historic Union Hotel, where in the late 1800s dances attracted revelers from Bodega, Freestone, Valley Ford, Sebastopol, and even Santa Rosa. The highest railroad bridge west of the Mississippi was located near here at the time. It was said of the early town, "It lies in the heart of a redwood forest, and the old stumps still stand in the streets." Evidence of early Italian settlement is still apparent with the flourishing of Neapolitan restaurants in town.

Also pictured in my drawing is the 1903 Church of St. Philip.

Occidental, Sonoma County

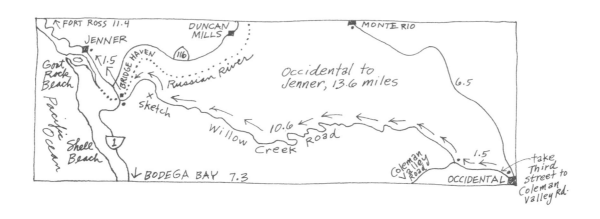

I drive the partly unpaved route to Jenner along
Willow Creek Road. It is winding and heavily forested
at times. Cattle chew their cuds and swat
flies with their tails as they lounge among
big ferns in the shade of a redwood grove.
A hawk and a raven swoop and clash with each
other in the sky above.
I draw a farmhouse nestled in a valley
near the coast where Willow Creek
flows into the Russian River.

Willow Creek farm, Sonoma County

Sweetwater landscape, Sonoma County

Roundabout to Armstrong State Park

Westside Road gives views of lush farm country and the
thick green of grapevines growing in the summer sun.
At Sweetwater Springs turnoff, I sketch a view of a
triple-stack hop kiln with Mt. St. Helena in the distance.

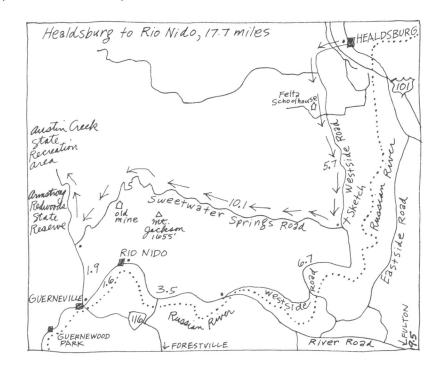

Hops, used as flavoring for beer, were a major crop in this area at one time. The long vines were hung to dry in these decorative buildings. The hop kilns are now used for a winery.

Sweetwater Springs Road has a primitive feel to it. Skirting Mount Jackson, it undoubtedly was made with a great deal of effort by early road builders. It twists and turns and is a bit steep and narrow—a more adventurous trip than merely continuing around the mountain on Westside Road. For those wishing an effortless, yet scenic route to Armstrong State Park, stay on Westside.

At Armstrong, ancient live redwoods may be viewed.

Back road to Fort Ross

From the wooded hamlet of Cazadero, Fort Ross Road winds up and over the coastal mountains. A fire had charred the landscape a few years back; however, the slow regeneration of the forest is now in process. Burned redwoods are striking new branches and seedling firs are sprouting new spring needles. Closer to the sea, purple iris blooms in quantity. At Fort Ross, a brisk, cool breeze blows across the bluffs where I choose to sketch.

Fort Ross, Sonoma County

At the Visitors' Center and bookstore you can learn the history of the old Russian fort, which has been extensively restored. In 1834 the Chief Ruler of the Russian Colonies in America had described it like this: "There have been erected two towers with cannons defending all sides of this so-called fort, which appears to the eyes of the Indians and local Spaniards, however, as being very strong and possibly even unconquerable. Within the enclosure... stand... the home of the director..., barracks, stores, and a chapel, kept in cleanliness and order... outside the fort... are located two company cattle barns, spacious and distinctively clean, with pens, a small building for storing milk and making butter, a shed for the Indians, a threshing floor, and two rows of small company and private homes with gardens and orchards.... In a clearing... stands a windmill...at a wharf for canoes are a broad shed and trading station, a blacksmithery, a tannery, and a bath house."

SAWS - SHARPENED

R.L. Shy
PHONE
963-3267 SCISSORS
KNIVES - TOOLS - SHARPENED
Carpenter and Cabinet Work

Back road sign,
Sonoma County

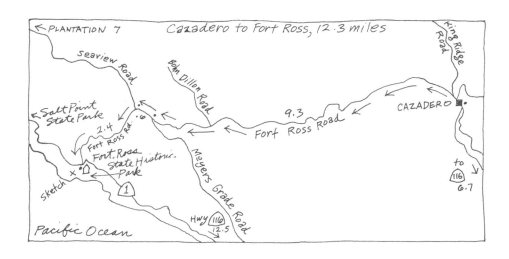

Cazadero to Fort Ross, 12.3 miles

← PLANTATION 7

Seaview Road

Bohn Dillon Road

King Ridge Road

Salt Point State Park

2.4

Fort Ross Rd.

.6

9.3

Fort Ross Road

CAZADERO

Fort Ross State Historic Park

Sketch

Meyers Grade Road

to 116
6.7

1

Pacific Ocean

Hwy 116
12.5

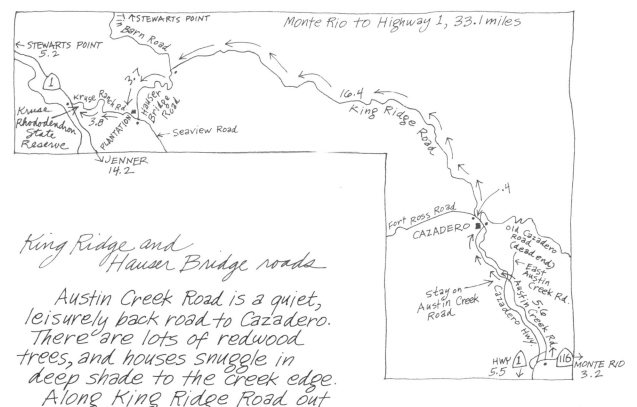

Monte Rio to Highway 1, 33.1 miles

↑ STEWARTS POINT

Barn Road

← STEWARTS POINT 5.2

1

Kruse Ranch Rd.

3.7

Hauser Bridge Road

16.4

King Ridge Road

Kruse Rhododendron State Reserve

3.8

PLANTATION

← Seaview Road

JENNER 14.2

.4

Fort Ross Road

CAZADERO

Old Cazadero Road (dead end)

← East Austin Creek Rd.

stay on Austin Creek Road

Austin Creek Rd.

5.6

Cazadero Hwy.

HWY 1
5.5 ↓

116 → MONTE RIO
3.2

King Ridge and Hauser Bridge roads

Austin Creek Road is a quiet, leisurely back road to Cazadero. There are lots of redwood trees, and houses snuggle in deep shade to the creek edge. Along King Ridge Road out of Cazadero, long views of the coastal mountain chain are outlined. It is grazing land and the road winds like an old cattle trail, skirting ancient wooden fencing and traversing the crests of dun-colored mountaintops. Hauser Bridge Road then dips down to where a narrow steel bridge crosses the picturesque Gualala River, then up and over another ridge and down to Plantation.

Plantation had a post office and a hotel in earlier days; it is now a private children's camp. As I sketch the Plantation barn, several cars emerge from Kruse Rhododendron State Reserve, their occupants stopping to ask, "Where am I" and "Where are the rhododendrons?"

The rhododendron's rose-tinted blooms appear between March and June. (This was a hot July day.) I proceed through the Reserve after leaving Plantation and note great clumps of rhododendrons disguised as green leaves at this time of year. The redwoods had been logged in the 1890s, and in the 1000-year cycle it takes to return to a redwood forest, the tanbark oak and rhododendron stage has been reached. Some tanbarks have been removed to keep from smothering out the colorful rhododendrons.

The white barn, Plantation, Sonoma County

The store at Stewarts Point, Sonoma County

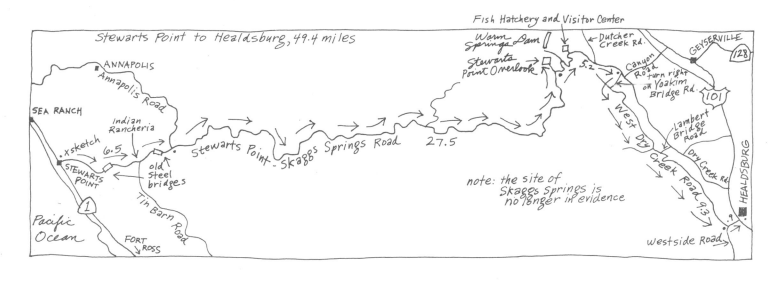

The Stewarts Point - Skaggs Springs Road

Opposite the quaint 1868 Stewarts Point store, the Stewarts Point-Skaggs Springs Road ascends through dense fir and redwood forest. An old steel bridge spans the Gualala River. I remember hoping that it wouldn't soon be replaced with the usual uninteresting modern concrete crossing. There is access to the river here and a possible picnicking spot.

I view ranges of coastal mountains as the road winds up and over various summits. Skaggs Springs was at one time a celebrated watering place which, in the 1860s, could accommodate 300 people. A writer of the time gave this description of the Springs: "There are here a few acres of tolerable, level fertile land; the rest of the country is pretty slanting; in fact up edgeways, and they pasture goats on both sides of it. There are plenty of deer in the vicinity, but it is very dangerous hunting them; if you should kill one it would be liable to fall on your head."

The road eventually becomes wider and faster as I approach the Warm Springs Dam and Fish Hatchery area. The Stewarts Point Overlook affords a dramatic view of the dam.

I take West Dry Creek Road down a narrow valley planted with grapevines to Highway 101 and Healdsburg.

Back roads
in apple country

Apple orchards pattern
the up-and-down
hills west of Sebastopol,
although new housing
and new vineyards have
downed a number of
trees in this picturesque
countryside.

apples near
Sebastopol,
Sonoma County

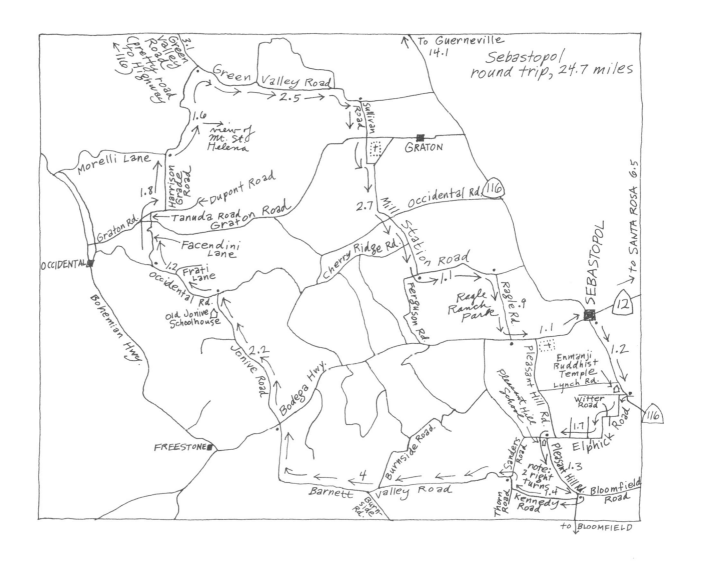

The main town, Sebastopol, was named for the Crimean port in the USSR. In the late 1800s it was famous as the birthplace of canned applesauce. An architectural tour of Sebastopol has been published by the Western Sonoma Historical Society, P.O. Box 816, Sebastopol. It includes a temple, which had traveled in toto from Japan to the Chicago World's Fair (1933-34) and then home to Sebastopol.

The rolling hills and winding roads take me through a varied landscape—from apple-growing areas to deep valleys and meadows. Apple trees give way to oaks and eucalyptus. Along Jonive Road are firs and redwoods and on Harrison Grade I drive past juniper and manzanita before returning to apple country and Sebastopol.

Back roads to the Napa Valley

In the deep shade of its garden I sketch Lachryma Montis (Tears of the Mountain), once the home of General Mariano Guadalupe Vallejo. It was named for the spring that supplied water to both the farm and the early town of Sonoma. In town I stop at the Sonoma League for Historic Preservation, 129 East Spain, to pick up its good walking guide to the town.

I travel the back roads from here into Napa County's Carneros district. Here, near the upper reaches of San Francisco Bay, the climate is cooler. It is a good place to plant wine grapes of the early maturing variety.

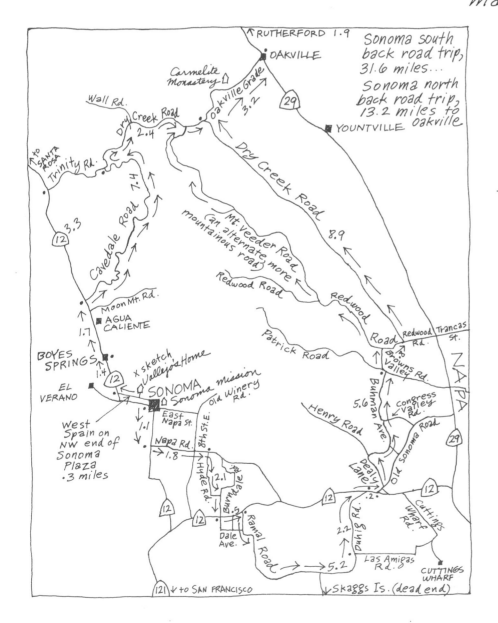

North of Sonoma, I look for Cavedale Road. It winds up into the Mayacamas Range with good views of Sonoma Valley. Toyon, maple, madrone, oak, bay, and fir trees seem to close in over the road. Joining Trinity Road, I travel over the mountains toward Oakville, stopping to enjoy an expansive view of Napa Valley.

Lachryma Montis, Sonoma County

Back road to Middletown

I pass Mark West Springs, where mineral hot springs were discovered in 1857. It had become a popular spa in the 19th century, famous for its sulphur baths. Ancient grapevines twine over the road at this point.

Franz Valley Road winds over the crest of the Mayacamas Range and drops into Franz Valley with a distant view of Mount St. Helena.

I reach Knights Valley, named for Thomas Knight who came to California in 1845. By 1853 Knight had earned enough money, possibly in mining for gold, to purchase a large portion of the valley and become a successful farmer. Ida Clayton Road was named to commemorate the pretty and popular teacher at Knights Valley School.

Massive and majestic Mt. St. Helena, at 4338 feet, rises almost twice as high as surrounding mountains. The most romantic fable of its naming follows that Helena de Gagarin, wife of the Governor-General of the Russian colonies in America, headed an expedition that ascended the mountain on June 20, 1841. At the top she christened it St. Helena in honor of the patron saint of the Empress of Russia.

Mt. St. Helena,
Sonoma County

39

Back road to Middletown

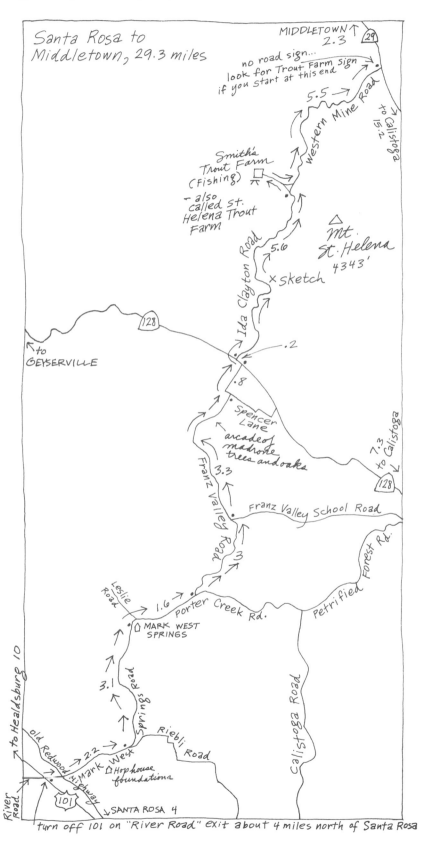

Santa Rosa to
Middletown, 29.3 miles

MIDDLETOWN ↑
2.3 [29]

no road sign...
look for Trout Farm sign
if you start at this end

5.5 →

western Mine Road

to Calistoga
15.2

Smith's
Trout Farm
(Fishing)

– also
called St.
Helena Trout
Farm

△
Mt.
St. Helena
4343'

5.6

× sketch

[128]

← to
GEYSERVILLE

.2

.8

Spencer
Lane

arcade of
madrone
trees and oaks

7.3
to Calistoga

[128]

3.3

Franz Valley School Road

Franz Valley Road

3

Petrified Forest Rd.

Leslie
Road

1.6 → Porter Creek Rd.

△ MARK WEST
SPRINGS

Calistoga Road

3.1

Mark West Springs Road

Riebli
Road

← to Healdsburg 10

old Redwood Highway

2.2 →

△ Hop house
foundations

River
Road

[101]

↓ SANTA ROSA 4

turn off 101 on "River Road" exit about 4 miles north of Santa Rosa

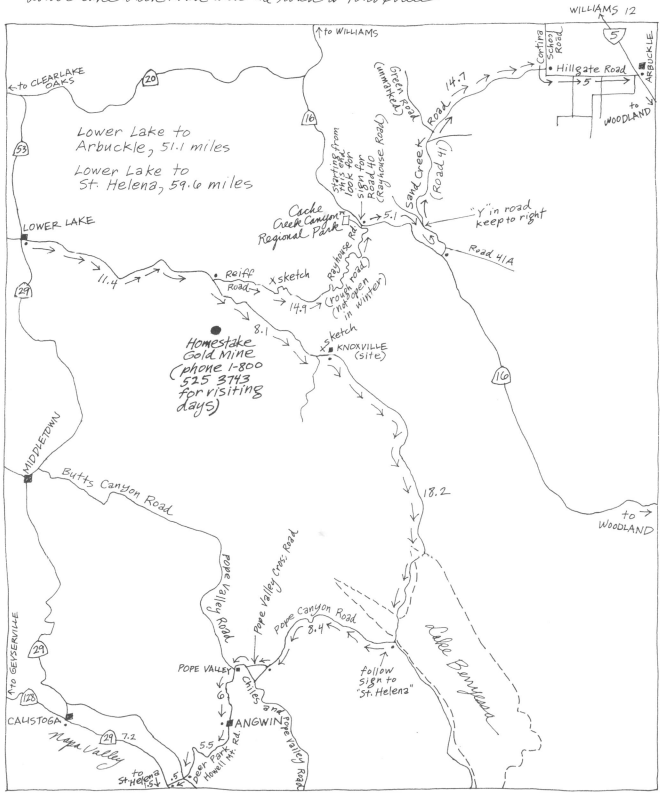

to WILLIAMS

WILLIAMS 12

to CLEARLAKE OAKS

20

16

Cortina School Road

5

Hillgate Road

ARBUCKLE

to WOODLAND

Green Road (unmarked)

Road 14.7

5

53

Lower Lake to
Arbuckle, 51.1 miles

Lower Lake to
St. Helena, 59.6 miles

starting from this end, look for sign for Road 40 (Rayhouse Road)

Sand Creek

(Road 41)

"Y" in road
keep to right

Cache
Creek Canyon
Regional Park

5.1

Road 41A

LOWER LAKE

11.4

29

Reiff
Road

x sketch

Rayhouse Rd.

(rough road)
(not open
in winter)

14.9

8.1

Homestake
Gold Mine
(phone 1-800
525 3743
for visiting
days)

x sketch

KNOXVILLE
(site)

16

MIDDLETOWN

Butts Canyon Road

18.2

to
WOODLAND

to GEYSERVILLE

Pope Valley Road

Pope Valley Cross Road

Lake Berryessa

29

Pope Canyon Road

8.4

128

Pope Valley

Chiles and Pope Valley Road

follow
sign to
"St. Helena"

CALISTOGA

ANGWIN

Napa Valley

29 7.2

.9

5.5

Deer Park

Howell Mt. Rd.

to
St. Helena
.5

.5

.5

41

Back road from Lower Lake

Lower Lake has a colorful mining town look to it. The 1868 IOOF building and the old jail still stand, as does the bulky brick 1877 schoolhouse—with a museum open to the public and a second-story former dance hall.

Morgan Valley Road heads east from here through farm country and into steeper hills where blue-green oaks and black-barked serpentine pines predominate.

Reiff Road goes east into Yolo County through the Blue Ridge Mountains to Highway 16 and Cache Creek Regional Park. I stop at the Reiff Ranch to sketch a barn built by the family in 1930. Mr. Reiff talks of fixing the structure because the mudsills, which had been its foundation, are gone and barn supports have gone askew. We agree that all a well-built barn needs is good roofing and a proper foundation and it will last forever. The road from here to Highway 16 bumps and joggles. It is a slow-going back road (and "closed during winter," a sign reports). I pass old, rusty mining buildings and, at another point, enjoy dramatic views of rugged mountains. Road 41 (Sand Creek Road) affords scenic views of the fertile valley far below. And, on topping the ridge, a view of mountains and hills, superimposed one on the next, extends as far as the eye can see.

Reiff Barn,
Lake County

43

The road to Knoxville (map, page 41)

In July grassy slopes shimmer with soft, golden light. Groves of oak trees make blue-green silhouettes on the hillsides and canyons.

At Knoxville I sketch the ghostly Manhattan Quicksilver Mine Headquarters building. Several 14-inch, spotted, black and tan alligator lizards eye me at close range and I shoo off the fierce-looking creatures with my drawing pad. Unusually curious, they return again and again, enjoying my little game.

South of Knoxville, Lake Berryessa gleams bright blue contrasting with the surrounding dun-colored hills.

Note: The Manhattan Quicksilver Mine Office pictured here is gone. Knoxville is returned to hill and pasture. Nary a stone marks the site.

46   *Round Valley Church, Covelo, Mendocino County*

Back road through Mendocino National Forest

This forest was conserved for the nation by President Theodore Roosevelt in 1907. Highway 162 from Willows continues just a few miles north of Elk Creek, climbing high into brush-covered mountains. I stopped to look at Grindstone Canyon and read a forest service sign pointing out brush clearance projects. Grass is planted for the deer and cow populations, instead of allowing brush to proliferate.

Up higher I am in a vast conifer forest with views of adjoining mountain ranges. As I proceed further the land opens up with more grazing areas. Views are often magnificent.

I reach Covelo in Round Valley and draw the Methodist Church. A squirrel looks out of the faded pink and white bell tower while woodpeckers fly back and forth adding new acorn holes to it. A poster in the church entrance announces that in a few days the church will host a free movie, "The Horror of Dracula."

Elk Creek to Covelo, 57.2 miles

The road to Blocksburg

North of Garberville, in the Avenue of the Giants, I draw an almost 8-foot-wide redwood stump. Over the years countless initials have been carved in the wood. One carving is somewhat more profound than the others. It states "Thou art God."

Leaving the great redwoods, I travel inland through hilly forest and meadow. Big views of mountain scenery appear, sometimes on both sides of the road as I drive higher. They are awe-inspiring. I bypass Fort Seward, a military post in 1861.

Redwoods
Humboldt County

At Blocksburg I get permission to sketch the town's oldest barn and march across a field of thistles and manure piles to sit in the shade of an old fruit tree. At the time the barn was built the town had seven bars and two barbershops. It was a tanbark-collecting center from which the bark was hauled to a faraway tannery in Willits. Sheep raising was big also and there was some manganese ore mining. The old Mail Ridge Stage Route north from San Francisco passed through here when Mr. Blocksburgher, the town's namesake, had been a storekeeper and wool merchant.

From Bridgeville—also a stop on the old Mail Ridge Stage Route—I climb up a long, steep gravel road. The climb is worth it for I am now richly rewarded with vast mountain views. Metal barn roofs glisten in the distance. I pass the charming community of Freshwater on my journey to Eureka.

Blocksburg barn,
Humboldt County

51

The road to Blocksburg

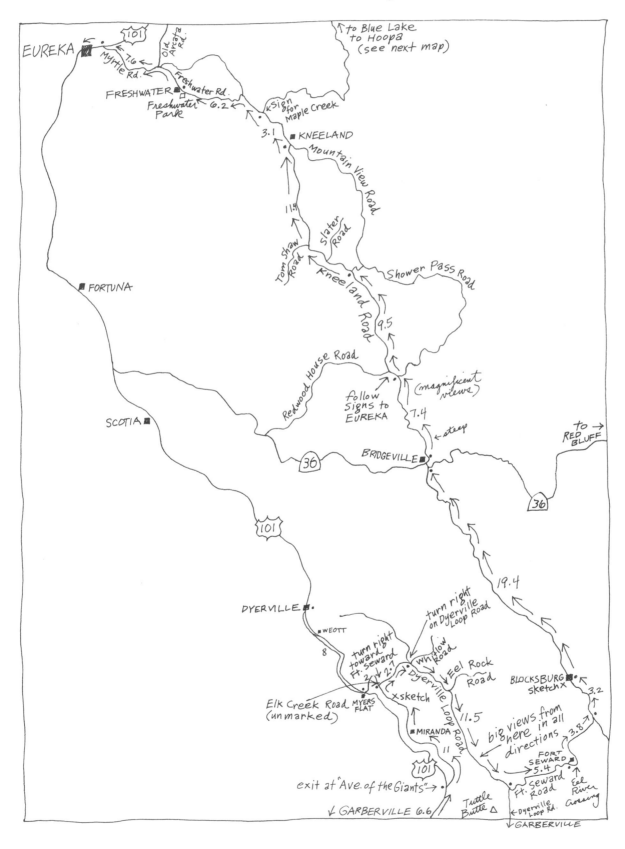

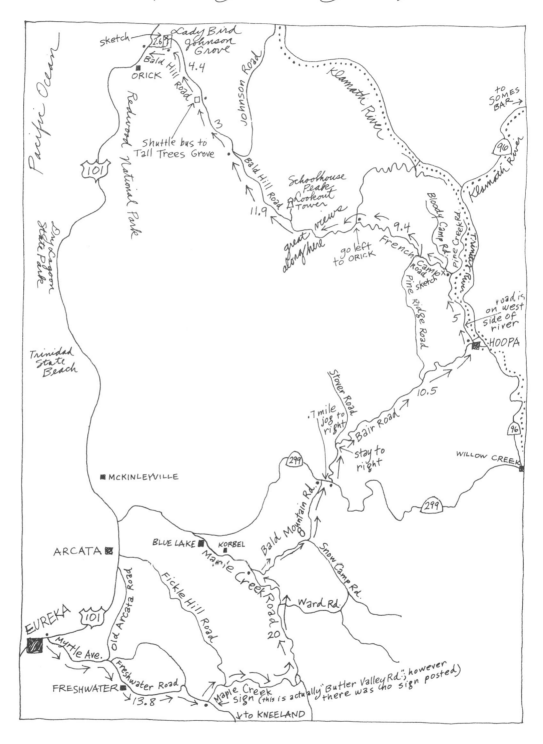

Hoopa Valley, Humboldt County 55

The road to Hoopa Valley — (map, page 53)

Butler Valley Road east of Eureka meanders north. A winding mountain road then proceeds across the Mad River and picturesque Maple Creek. Near Lord Ellis Summit, forest foliage joins overhead to become a tunnel of green. Firs, cedars, tanbark, oak, and madrone line Bair Road to Hoopa Valley. Leaving Hoopa, I sketch a view with the Klamath River glinting in the sun, winding its way through the green valley, fine mountain scenery all around. A madrone tree offers shade and drops stiff, dry leaves about me with each slight breeze.

Hoopa Valley to Lady Bird Johnson Grove (map, page 53)

The long pull uphill from Hoopa Valley finally emerges on top of the world (or so it seems!). The views exhilarate and lift the spirit. I travel through high pastureland and descend near the coast to Lady Bird Johnson Grove. There I draw a so-called Goose Pen Tree (redwood), which pioneers had, on occasion, used to confine small livestock and fowl. Oxalis, sword fern, salal, and evergreen huckleberry grow at its redwood base. Scarred by ancient fires, the tree itself remains alive and well, a giant in this truly magnificent stand of redwoods. Experiencing this place is enriching and inspiring.

Goose Pen redwood, Humboldt County

The Salmon Alps, Siskiyou County

Back road along the Salmon River to Scott Valley

From Somes Bar and Highway 96 and from Forks of
Salmon to Cecilville, a narrow, paved, winding, sometimes
one-way road clings to the rocky ledge high above
the roaring Salmon River. A sign early on had
warned motorists that slow travel and honking of
the horn on blind curves might be necessary.

Views of the Salmon Alps appear as I approach
Cecilville. From Cecilville the road becomes straighter
and smoother (and thereby less interesting). At the
Salmon Summit and the Pacific Crest Trailhead heliport
I sketch 7,790-foot Eagle Peak and include Billy's
Peak and Battle Mountain. They are all lined up in
splendid array from this scenic viewpoint.

I descend from here to Callahan at the foot of Scott Valley.

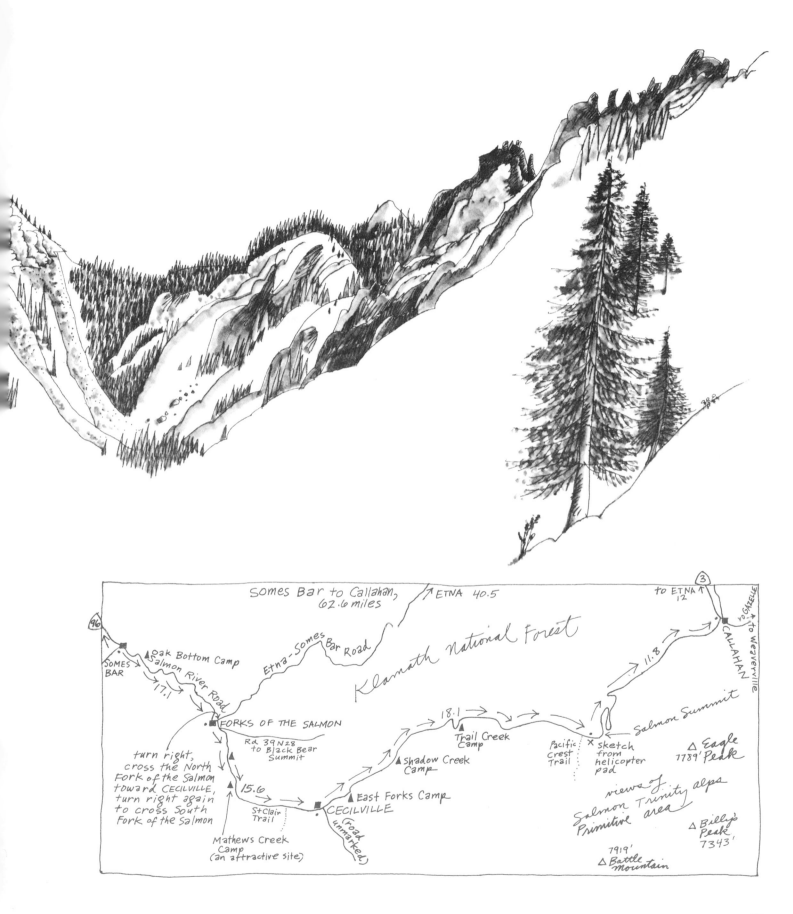

Somes Bar to Callahan, 62.6 miles

ETNA 40.5

Klamath National Forest

96

SOMES BAR

Oak Bottom Camp

Salmon River Road

Etna-Somes Bar Road

17.1

FORKS OF THE SALMON

Rd 39N28 to Black Bear Summit

turn right, cross the North Fork of the Salmon toward CECILVILLE, turn right again to cross South Fork of the Salmon

15.6

St Clair Trail

Mathews Creek Camp (an attractive site)

East Forks Camp

CECILVILLE (road unmarked)

Shadow Creek Camp

18.1

Trail Creek Camp

Pacific Crest Trail

x sketch from helicopter pad

Salmon Summit

11.8

to ETNA 12

3

CALLAHAN

to GAZELLE

to Weaverville

△ Eagle 7789' Peak

views of Salmon Trinity alps Primitive area

△ Billy's Peak 7343'

7919' △ Battle Mountain

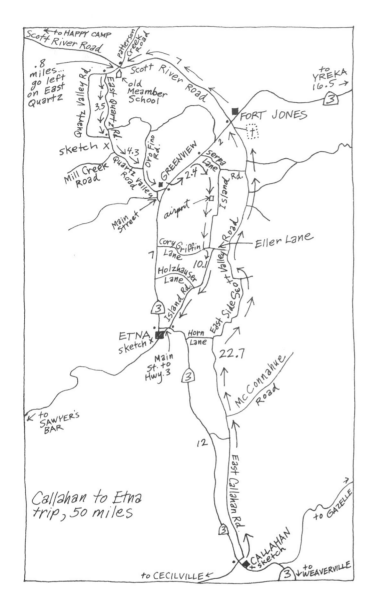

A trip through Scott Valley

The valley was named for John Scott, who had led a group of miners into the area in 1850. He discovered gold, and Scott Valley became a rich mining region. Today the valley is green with agricultural crops. Sprinklers sprinkle and black angus cows browse in the field.

In Quartz Valley, where gold camps once flourished, I sketch a neat, white schoolhouse and its monumental stone marker.

At Etna, originally known as Rough and Ready Mills, I draw the library building with its massive flagpole. As you approach the town, you can see the pole towering over all the other structures. I asked at the post office, city hall, and finally, a corner delicatessen to find out the height of the pole. The gentleman who told me it was 136½ feet (two feet shorter than the one at neighboring Fort Jones) wondered whether I wanted to climb it. I said no, but I'd enjoy seeing someone else do it!

QUARTZ VALLEY SCHOOL

White Schoolhouse, Siskiyou County

Etna's flagpole,
Siskiyou County

ETNA FREE LIBRARY and READING ROOM

Back road from Scott Valley

The Farrington Blacksmith Shop, the General Store, and the Ranch Hotel still stand at Callahan. I draw the old sign over the post office entrance next to the General Store and chat with the owner whose great-grandfather had built these historic edifices. In the 1860s this locality was a stage stop along the principal wagon road north to Oregon.

The road going east from Callahan rises gently to almost 5,000 feet through pine and cedar forest, then suddenly drops toward Interstate 5 near Gazelle.

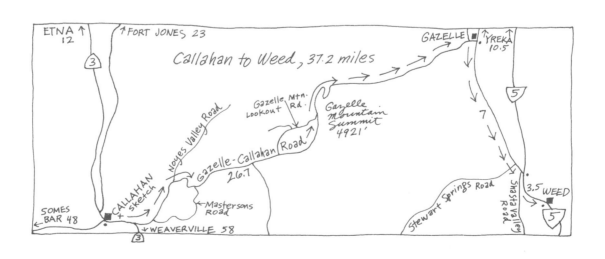

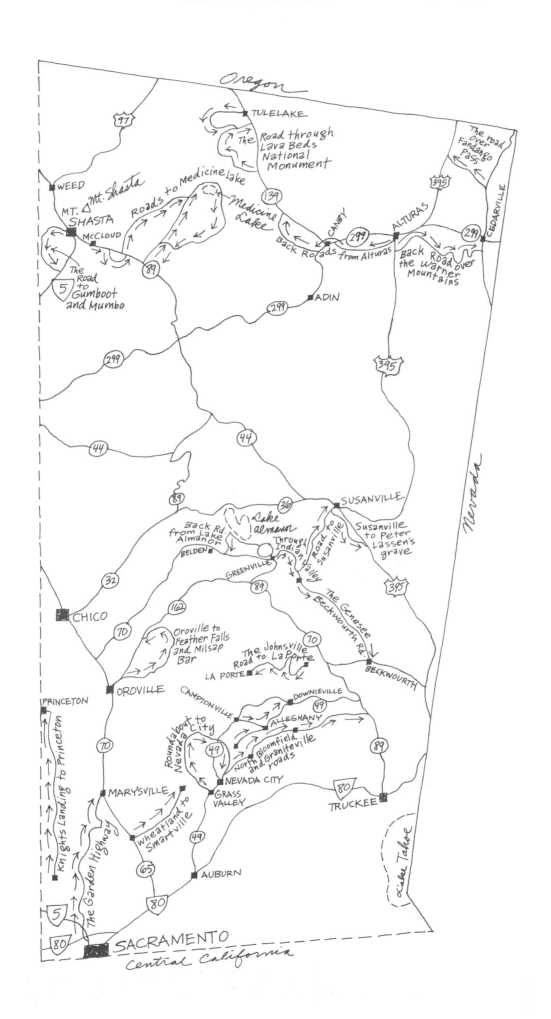

Oregon

TULELAKE

97

The Road through Lava Beds National Monument

The road over Fandango Pass

WEED

Mt. Shasta

MT. SHASTA

McCLOUD

Roads to Medicine Lake

Medicine Lake

139

395

CEDARVILLE

CANBY

ALTURAS

299

299

Back Roads from Alturas

Back Road over the Warner Mountains

5 The Road to Gumboot and Mumbo

89

ADIN

299

299

395

44

44

89

36

SUSANVILLE

Lake Almanor

Back Rd. from Lake Almanor

BELDEN

Through Indian Valley

Road to Susanville

Susanville to Peter Lassen's grave

32

GREENVILLE

89

395

CHICO

162

The Genesee

Beckwourth Rd.

70

Oroville to Feather Falls and Milsap Bar

The Johnsville Road to La Porte

70

LA PORTE

BECKWOURTH

PRINCETON

OROVILLE

CAMPTONVILLE

DOWNIEVILLE

49

Roundabout to Nevada City

ALLEGHANY

North Bloomfield and Graniteville roads

89

Knights Landing to Princeton

70

49

NEVADA CITY

80

MARYSVILLE

GRASS VALLEY

TRUCKEE

Wheatland to Smartville

49

Lake Tahoe

65

AUBURN

5

The Garden Highway

80

80

SACRAMENTO

Central California

64

Northeastern California

It is heartening to think that however loud the main arteries of traffic may become, there are back roads existing in quietude and natural beauty. I leave the insistent, fretful clamor of the freeway and travel the lonely back roads. Their untainted atmosphere and the closeness of trees and roadside flowers are of infinite attraction to me. It wouldn't be practical to pave or straighten these roads. They serve no profitable purpose, and for that I am thankful.

monkey flower, Placer County

Castle Crags, Siskiyou County

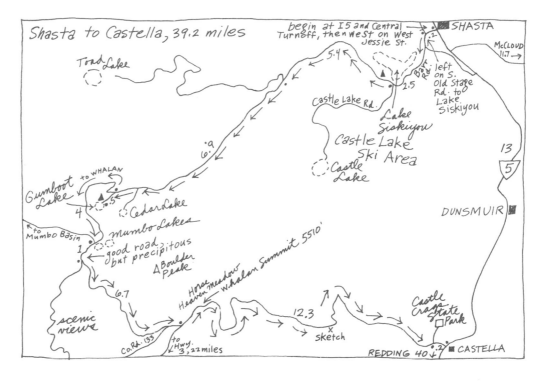

Shasta to Castella, 39.2 miles

begin at I5 and Central Turnoff, then west on West Jessie St. → SHASTA

McCLOUD 11.7 →

Toad Lake

5.4

left on S. Old Stage Rd. to Lake Siskiyou

Barr Rd.

2.5

Castle Lake Rd.

Lake Siskiyou

Castle Lake Ski Area

Castle Lake

13

5

DUNSMUIR

.9

6.9

to WHALAN

Gumboot Lake

4

.5

Cedar Lake

Mumbo Lakes

to Mumbo Basin

1

good road but precipitous

Boulder Peak

Horse Heaven Meadow

Whalan Summit 5510'

Castle Crags State Park

6.7

scenic views

Co. Rd. 133

to Hwy. 3, 22 miles

12.3

sketch

REDDING 40

.2

CASTELLA

The road to Gumboot and Mumbo

I pass tranquil Lake Siskiyou and ascend the rugged, rocky canyon. A rushing stream tumbles and splashes downward on my left. Gumboot Lake, cradled in granite in this high mountain wilderness, deeply reflects the blue of the sky. There are views near Mumbo Lake of far distant mountain ranges of northern California, including the high Trinity Alps. Finally I see the impressive Castle Crags and stop to draw its soft gray-colored prominence in the early morning light. It has been a fine trip for the beauty of mountain places, long views, and impressive high country forests.

Roads to Medicine Lake

The trip to Medicine Lake begins with stops to view McCloud River Falls. Upper and Lower Falls are easy enough to find; Middle Falls, however, is not marked. The roar can be heard from the roadway, so I follow the sound. There is a sheer cliff to be wary of and therefore this is no place for small children. All three falls are well worth viewing as they churn over rock ledges with a resounding roar. But Middle and Upper Falls are the most dramatic.

There are three routes from the McCloud area to Medicine Lake. Route 13, the road I follow, affords closer views of Mt. Shasta.

I see Paint Pot Crater, just visible from the road at one point, then Pumice Mountain. On Medicine Lake Road I pass at the very foot of Little Glass Mountain where great black chunks of obsidian glisten in the sunshine.

Back road musician,
Lower Falls, Siskiyou County

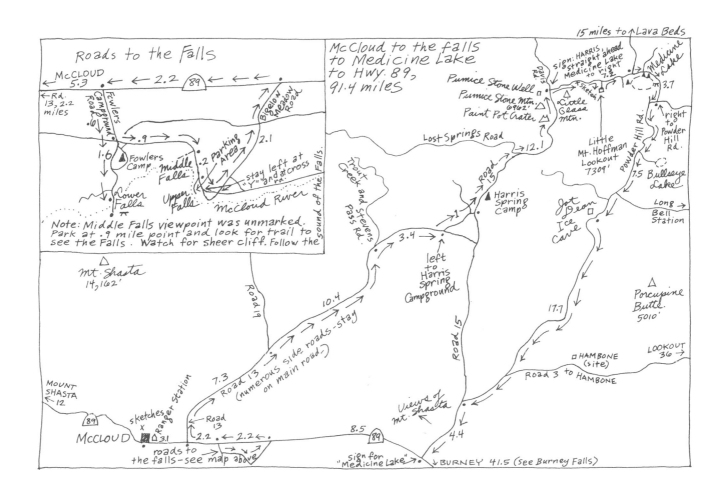

Roads to the Falls

McCLOUD ← 2.2 (89) ←
5.3
←Rd.
13, 2.2
miles

Fowlers Campground Road

Bigelow Meadow Road

.9   parking area   2.1

1.6   Fowlers Camp   Middle Falls   .2   "stay left at "Y" and cross rd."

Lower Falls   Upper Falls   McCloud River   sound of the Falls

Note: Middle Falls viewpoint was unmarked. Park at .9 mile point and look for trail to see the Falls. Watch for sheer cliff. Follow the

McCloud to the falls
to Medicine Lake
to Hwy. 89,
91.4 miles

sign: HARRIS
straight ahead
Medicine Lake
to right   7.2

Davis Rd.

Pumice Stone Well   Medicine Lake
Pumice Stone Mtn.
6962'   Little Glass mtn.   3.7
Paint Pot Crater

Lost Springs Road   12.1   right to Powder Hill Rd.

Trout Creek and Stevens Pass Rd.   Road 13   Little Mt. Hoffman Lookout 7309'   Powder Hill Rd.   7.5 Bullseye Lake

Harris Spring Camp   Jot Dean Ice Cave   Long Bell Station

.1   3.4   left to Harris Spring Campground   △ Porcupine Butte 5010'

mt. Shasta
14,162'

Road 19

10.4   Road 13
(numerous side roads-stay on main road-)   Road 15   17.7   □ HAMBONE (site)   LOOKOUT 36 →

7.3   Road 13 to HAMBONE

MOUNT SHASTA ← 12   Ranger Station   sketches   Road 13   Views of mt. Shasta   4.4

(89)   x   △ 3.1
McCLOUD   2.2 ← 2.2   8.5   (89)

roads to the falls-see map above   sign for "Medicine Lake" →   ↓BURNEY 41.5 (see Burney Falls)

I stop to sketch a particularly dramatic view of Mount Shasta, the helter-skelter profile of Little Glass Mountain in the middle distance. At Little Mount Hoffman lookout a 360-degree view of the world is presented below. The less-than-a-mile drive to the lookout, though precipitous, should be done.

The view of the entire Little Glass Mountain lava flow is particularly interesting from this point.

Medicine Lake proves a lovely, protected, bright blue body of water, and there's a good view of it from the picnic grounds. You have the option of either going further to see Lava Beds National Monument or returning toward McCloud. Jot Dean Ice Cave is on the way to McCloud. It has its own mystic sense of beauty with subtle colorings and dripping sound effects.

Mount Shasta, Siskiyou County

In McCloud I explore
the streets of this
quaint company town.
I travel out East
Columbero, go north
on Shasta and east
on Mill Street.
    Past the big mill
I follow Firenze
Street and North
Street back to the
mill. Following West
Columbero, I take
Hennessy Way to
Tucci, Walnut, and
Oak. I draw the
Bradshaw House,
former lumber
executive residence
near Lawndale Court
off Main, and the
log church. It
    occurs to me that
    the chocolate brown
    church with its
    whipped cream
    colored seams
    actually looks quite
    appetizing.

The Bradshaw House, McCloud,
    Siskiyou County

72

St. Joseph's, the chocolate brown church,
McCloud, Siskiyou County

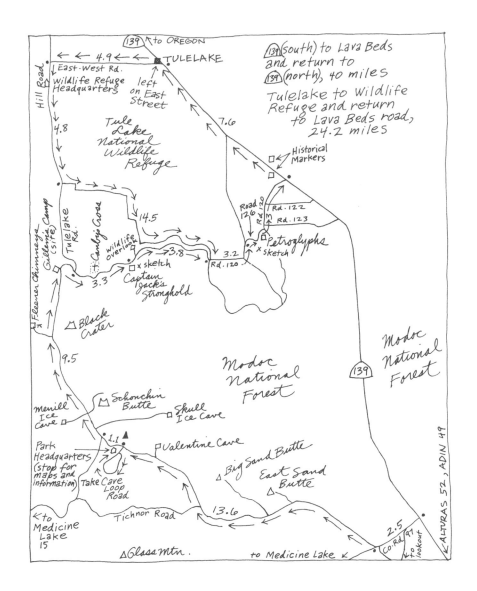

The road through Lava Beds National Monument

There are 20 caves to explore within 3 miles of the
Visitors' Center. Mushpot Cave is well lit, but flashlights
are a necessity for the others. They have colorful names
which invite exploration, like Golden Dome, Hopkins
Chocolate, and Hercules Leg.

I sketch at Captain Jack's Stronghold, where the
Modoc tribe made the U.S. Army pay dearly for victory
over the intransigent Indians. As I walk the path
through the stronghold I realize how 60 rugged Indians
could hold back an army of 600 for five months.

Captain Jack's Stronghold,
Siskiyou and Modoc Counties   77

If it's not too late in the day and you're not in a rush to go on, you could double back to the Tulelake Road (see map) and take the Wildlife Tour Route back to Lava Beds Monument. Otherwise, it might be best to stay overnight in Tulelake and leave the Wildlife Tour for the next day, which is what I decide to do.

At the Petroglyphs I sketch ancient markings, enjoying their simple designs. I watch swallows flying around their mud nests.

On the Wildlife Tour I see ducks of all sorts, herons, white pelicans, Canadian geese, varieties of seabirds, thousands of shiny blue dragonflies, locusts, bees, and a lively assortment of unnamed creatures.

Petroglyphs, Lava Beds National Monument, Modoc County

Back road over the Warner Mountains

I leave Alturas and stop at scenic Dorris Reservoir.
The surface of the reservoir is placid, the morning sun
glinting off the water. A flight of honking geese make
a "V" formation overhead. Grazing horses on a
nearby shore look like cutouts on the horizon.
The Warner Mountains in the distance, snow still
lingering on Squaw Peak, beckon me. The road
goes through juniper and pine forest, crosses
several streams, and gently ascends into the Warners.

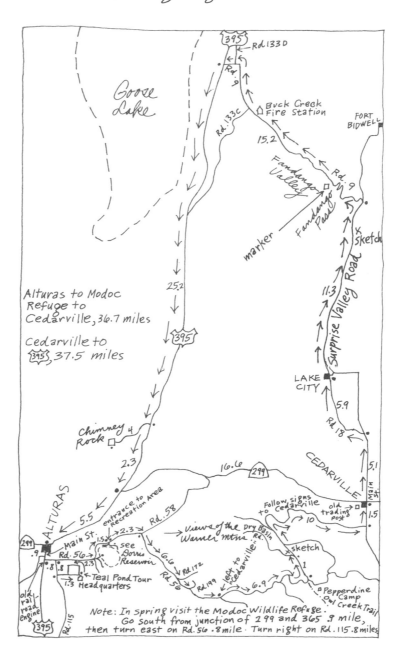

At the summit I draw a twisted and all but downed juniper. It expresses well the ferocity of winter storms at this altitude. Grasshoppers make clicking noises, an unseen bird sings, a cool light breeze whooshes through the pines, flies buzz, and range cattle come to stare at me.

From this point the road levels off, then descends toward Cedarville in Surprise Valley. Wagon trains came through here in the 1860s, and James Townsend built a trading post in 1865. He was killed by Indians in 1866. William Cressler and John Bonner bought the Townsend building in 1867 and turned it into a combination trading post and store. What is left of it can still be seen in the town park on Center Street between Highway 299 and Bonner Street.

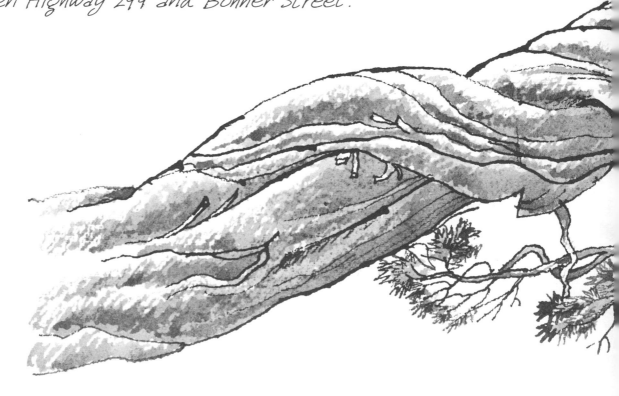

Twisted Juniper,
Warner Mountains, Modoc County

The road over Fandango Pass (see map, page 79)

I travel from Cedarville to the hamlet of Lake City, enjoying sweeping views of Surprise Valley and Upper Lake. Early pioneers were surprised to find a green valley after leaving the barren landscape of Nevada; thereby the name, Surprise Valley. I sketch the inventive antelope and deer horn arrangement at the Hanks Ranch and talk to a charming 88-year-old ranch woman who looks every bit the pioneer in big, floppy hat and one-piece dress. Her gnarled hands point to some cows and calves moving past. She is worried about the whereabouts of a particular calf.

HANKS ◦ RANCH

Back road ranch sign, Modoc County

The approach to Fandango is steep. The Peter Lassen and Applegate trails come together here, then part again on the other side of the Warners. Lassen goes south, Applegate north. A massacre took place along this trail sometime between 1846 and 1850. It is said that Indians attacked while pioneers were dancing the fandango. The fandangoists were completely wiped out. Today I enjoy the sweeping view across Fandango Valley; cows grazing on the opposite side look like slowly moving specks.

Back Roads from Alturas

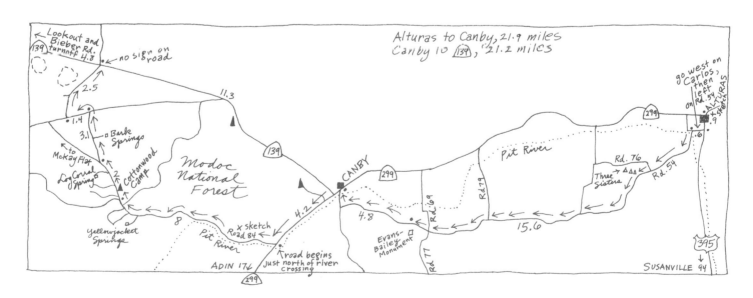

The Court House, Alturas, Modoc County

Back roads of Alturas — (map, page 83)

Before leaving Alturas, I admire the solidly elegant bulk of the Modoc County Court House. To sketch it I gain permission to sit on the lawn surrounding the chalk white golden-domed building. 1914 is the date on its facade, and F. J. DeLongchamps was the architect. Niles Hotel is another notable building in Alturas.

When you visit the Chamber of Commerce you are in the original County Recorder Office of Modoc County. To the rear is the old jail.

I travel the Centerville Road west and enjoy broad views of agricultural land and juniper forest. Yellow daisies line the roadway at times, pretty faces turned to the morning sun.

On a hill to the south a white marker commemorates the death of S.D. Evans and Joe Bailey, killed by Indians in July 1861 while driving 900 head of beef cattle to the mines in Virginia City, Nevada.

NAVY ITS NOT JUST A JOB ITS AN ADVENTURE

GO AIR FORCE

USAF REC OFFICE

Going west I reach Canby, named for
the U.S. General of the Modoc War, and
turn left to locate County Road 84 and
the Pit River. I enjoy the scenery along
the lazily flowing stream and pause to
draw one of the views. Cows scratching their
backs on low juniper branches stop to moo.
Only two cowboys in pickup trucks pass
in one and a half hours. The road has
the essence of an old covered wagon trail.
(map, page 83)

The Pit River, Modoc County

Back road from Lake Almanor

The road hugs the shore of Butt Valley
Reservoir. It is a pretty body of water despite
the eye-jarring power-line structures. I cross
the dam spillway and proceed down toward
the rushing Feather River. What a colossal
canyon! I descend steep slopes with
views of forested mountainsides and
clouds feathering out along mountain
tops. At Caribou, an attractive PG&E
Company village, there is a sign,
"Fishermen Welcome." I picnic nearby
with a view of the Forebay and the impressive cliffs opposite. I continue along
the road, stopping to watch a gold-sluicing
operation in
the river. The
road ends at
Highway 70
near Belden
town and the
Eby Stamp
Mill road-
side rest.

Road block,
Plumas County

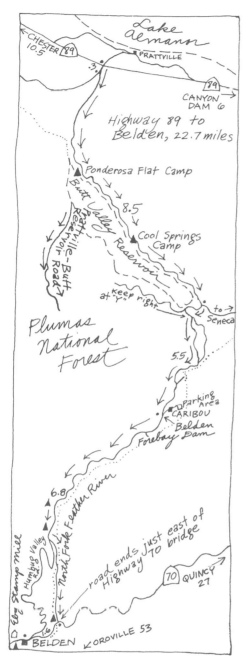

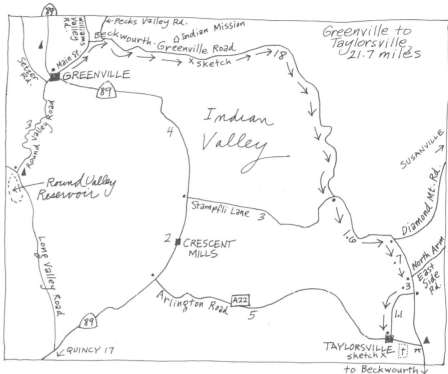

Back road through Indian Valley

I travel from Greenville, long a center of quartz mining activity. It has a distinctive California mining and lumber town look about it. The place is located at one end of broad and beautiful Indian Valley. In winter there are views of surrounding snow-capped peaks. I stop to sketch Wheelock Shingle Mill with Mount Hough and Grizzly Peak in the background. The old mill has since been virtually destroyed by heavy snows.

The old Wheelock Shingle Mill,
Indian Valley, Plumas County

91

At Taylorsville I search the
pioneer cemetery for the monument
marking the grave of the town's namesake, Jobe
Taylor, who settled here in 1852. (I find it.)
This is a village of quaint rural charm with
old houses along shady streets, a white
steepled church, and many barns.

Taylorsville Community Church, 1875

Crescent Mills roundabout to Taylorsville,
or on to Susanville

I sketch a barn full of wood along the way
at a ranch homesteaded by the James B. Peter family.

Crescent
Mills to
Susanville,
34.8 miles

HWY 47 89
44
6
SUSANVILLE
Gold Run Rd.
4.5
4
36
to ALTURAS 94
395

Lake almanor 38
36
Rd. to Moonlight V.
Rd. to Fleming Sheep Camp
Peter Lassen grave
9
395

Rd. to Westwood
15.4
road quality on the primitive side
JANESVILLE

Rd. to Morton Creek

Road to Snake Cabin

Road to Moonlight Valley

Road to Antelope Lake

3 roads come together take road on left to Susanville

Engle Mine ruins
5.4

CANYON DAM 9

Antelope Lake

sketch x
5
North Arm East Side Rd.

GREENVILLE 4 89

Diamond Mtn. Road

x sketch 6.2

Stampfli Lane

CRESCENT MILLS
4.5

Note: This is an alternate drive back to Taylorsville if you elect not to drive the sometimes primitive road to Susanville.

TAYLORSVILLE

QUINCY 23

BECKWOURTH

Peter Ranch barn near Taylorsville,
Plumas County

The North Arm of Indian Valley is a grand, green expanse bounded by forested mountains.

I draw the valley in the silent, sunny morning. Ants crawl up my legs, bees hum, and the work of woodpeckers echoes across the valley.

You can return to Indian Valley via North Arm East Side Road at the valley's end.

I choose to go over the mountains to Susanville. The road is paved, but steep in places; eventually the pine forest thins out, and I descend to the pleasant farming country around Susanville.

The North Arm of Indian Valley, Plumas County

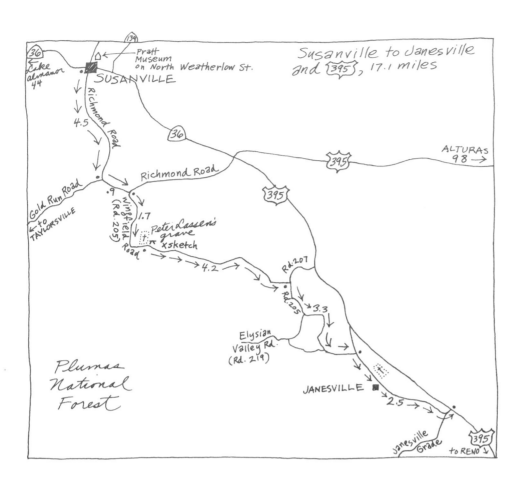

Pratt
Museum
on North Weatherlow St.

SUSANVILLE

Susanville to Janesville
and 395, 17.1 miles

36
Lake
almanor
44

Richmond Road

4.5

36

Richmond Road

395

ALTURAS
98 →

Gold Run Road
to TAYLORSVILLE

.9

Winfield
Road
(Rd.205)

1.7

395

Peter Lassen's
grave
× sketch

4.2

Rd.207

Rd.205

3.3

Elysian
Valley Rd.
(Rd.219)

Plumas
National
Forest

JANESVILLE

2.5

Janesville Grade

395

to RENO ↓

Susanville to Peter Lassen's grave and Janesville

Isaac Roop was the first white settler in Honey Lake Valley. Susanville, in fact, was named for his first daughter. The Roop log cabin still stands in the city park on Weatherlow Street as does the Lassen Historical Museum.

I travel from here to Peter Lassen's grave. Lassen came here from Denmark when he was 29, lived in Indian Valley for awhile and then settled in this area in 1855. Unfortunately, it may not have been a good choice since he was killed here by Indians on April 26, 1859, at age 66.

I sketch a decorative rail fence, to the harmonies of mooing cows, on my way to the interesting community of Janesville. A rancher, mending fences, stops long enough to shake his head and comment on my drawing: "Well, that's another way to earn a living, I guess."

Split rail fence near Susanville, Lassen County

The Genesee-Beckwourth Road

In Genesee Valley I find idyllic farm scenery with grazing cows and sheep, old barns, and old farms. There is still a good collection of buildings marking the former hamlet of Genesee. I continue on Beckwourth Road, crossing a creek full of big granite boulders at Drum Bridge. The landscape changes dramatically farther along when great lava outcroppings appear. The forest becomes sparse, and gray-green sagebrush patterns the landscape. I come across horses in the road. Then deer and fawns leap across the way.

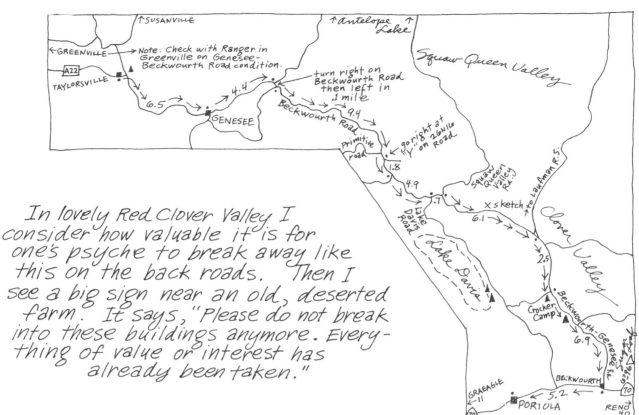

Note: Check with Ranger in Greenville on Genesee-Beckwourth Road condition.

In lovely Red Clover Valley I consider how valuable it is for one's psyche to break away like this on the back roads. Then I see a big sign near an old, deserted farm. It says, "Please do not break into these buildings anymore. Everything of value or interest has already been taken."

I despair that a sign like this is necessary. I then must rationalize that the people who buy my book and travel this road are those with a genuine feeling for history and nature who would protect what they see. I pass meadows with cows lying contentedly in them. There is no fencing. I view the striking Sugar Loaf Mountain and finally reach Beckwourth and Highway 70. Jim Beckwourth, trapper and scout, was the first to locate Beckwourth Pass, at 5,212 feet the lowest over the summit of the Sierras.

The Masonic Temple building is still standing in Beckwourth. There is also a general store and the colorful Beckwourth Tavern interior.

Red Clover Valley, Plumas County

102

Johnsville, Plumas County

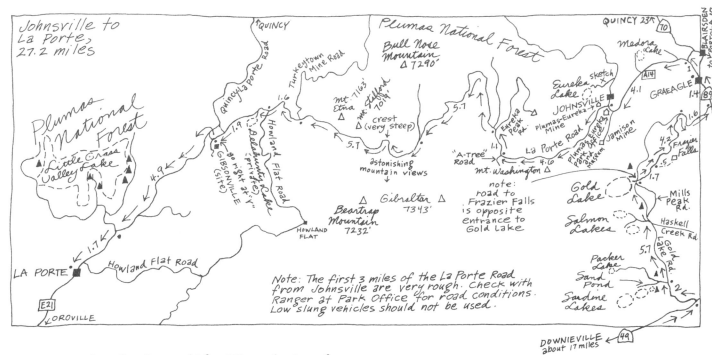

The Johnsville Road to La Porte

I travel Gold Lake Road to the fabled lake whose shoreline was supposedly covered with chunks of gold. This was according to a J.R. Stoddard, who had stumbled across such a lake, he said, somewhere between Downieville and Sierra Valley in 1849. It was never found, yet the name Gold Lake was given to this lovely body of water.

I take the road opposite the lake to Frazier Falls. A ½-mile hike takes me to a good view of the 248-foot cascade of water. Graeagle is close by and so are the old mining town of Johnsville and Plumas-Eureka State Park.

I stop to draw Johnsville and Mount Washington from the road to Eureka Lake. At the park museum are Snowshoe Thompson's 25-pound skis, which he used to carry the mail across the Sierras in wintertime. He did this for five years beginning in 1856, skiing from Placerville to Carson Valley, Nevada, and back. After a visit to the museum, I inspect portions of the nearby Plumas-Eureka mine, where millions of dollars in gold were produced.

"The first three miles are the bumpiest," I am told by the ranger at the State Park, as we discuss the road to La Porte. He's right. I drive at much less than ten miles per hour. I listen to a classical music station beaming Beethoven's Emperor concerto from Reno, Nevada. My spirit is filled with the beauty of it all. It should never be made an easier trip. I finally reach the crest of this high Sierra journey—a bit steep but maneuverable—and later pass the site of Gibsonville town on the road to La Porte.

Oroville to Feather Falls and Milsap Bar
(map, page 106)

Feather Falls is nicely unified in design with each building painted barn red with white trim. The place seems to be dismantling at this writing, however, perhaps one day becoming a ghost town.

Turning off the paved road onto the dusty one to Cascade, a man astride a small motorcycle approaches. He is the friendly owner of the Cascade Saloon, and I am intrigued enough by his description of the place to locate and draw it.

Electricity is generated with a large home-made waterwheel, so the "Bud" sign in the window is lit, and the drinks are cold. When my sketch was first made, the bottled gas containers you see in the picture had been the energy source. The saloon has been restored and is more colorful than ever.

The road to Milsap Bar is also called Hansen Bar Trail Road. You must check your mileage from Cascade so you do not miss the turnoff. It may be unmarked. The route is a primitive one and slow-going, a journey for the more adventurous. A passenger car can·make it at this writing, however, a 4-wheel drive vehicle would be preferable. (An alternate route from Cascade is to stay on the paved Hartman Bar Road to La Porte—perhaps free of snow by late May or June.)

Cascade Saloon,
Cascade, Plumas County

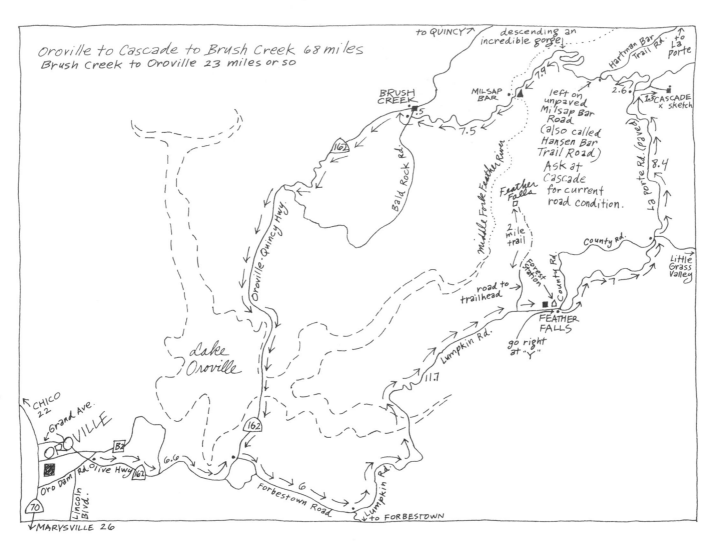

Oroville to Cascade to Brush Creek 68 miles
Brush Creek to Oroville 23 miles or so

to QUINCY

descending an incredible gorge!

Hartman Bar Trail Rd. to La Porte

7.9

2.6

BRUSH CREEK .5

MILSAP BAR

left on unpaved Milsap Bar Road (also called Hansen Bar Trail Road) Ask at Cascade for current road condition.

1.5 CASCADE x sketch

162

Bald Rock Rd.

7.5

La Porte Rd. (paved)

8.4

Middle Fork Feather River

Feather Falls

Oroville-Quincy Hwy.

2 mile trail

County Rd.

County Rd.

Little Grass Valley

Forest Station

7

road to trailhead

Lake Oroville

Lumpkin Rd.

FEATHER FALLS

go right at "Y"

CHICO 22

Grand Ave.

OROVILLE

11.7

162

70

Oro Dam Rd. Olive Hwy. 162

6.6

Lincoln Blvd.

6

Forbestown Road

Lumpkin Rd.

to FORBESTOWN

MARYSVILLE 26

The Garden Highway to Marysville and Yuba City

It is easy to get onto this road by simply coming off Interstate 5 at the Garden Highway sign just north of Sacramento. You are immediately on a levee road along the Feather River and on your way to Yuba City on the back roads.

Interesting and sometimes elegant houses line riverbanks screened by huge bushes of oleanders. There are good views of the river from time to time and of the rich farmland of the Sacramento delta region. Plums, walnuts, corn, peaches, and tomatoes are some of the crops planted. I stop along Scheiber Road to sketch one of the great farms, the "Circle S."

MARYSVILLE
YUBA CITY
.9 Feather River Blvd. entrance to freeway
Grand Ave.
12.5
Feather River
Feather River Blvd.
go left off 70 onto Feather River Blvd.
Bear River
Bear River Rd.
4
Garden Hwy. goes under Drescher Road (99)
Sketch 3.2
Cornelius Rd.
turn left on Scheiber Road (look sharp)
NICOLAUS
Marcum Road
Lee Rd.
Feather River 7.2
VERONA
Sankey Rd.
Riego Road
Sacramento River 9.3
Garden Highway
Power Line Rd.
Elverta Rd.
take Garden Highway turnoff and drive west
7.8
Garden
San Juan Rd
Hwy.
Garden Hwy. goes under 880
2.5
SACRAMENTO

Sacramento to Marysville 40.2m

Ranch near Nicolaus, Sutter County

WILLOWS 18 ↑
Road 67
PRINCETON ■
take ferry to Hwy 45
Road 69
also called Rd.xx
45
River Road
to COLUSA
Gridley Rd.
15.5
Sacramento River
River Road
Knights Landing to Princeton, 59.3 miles
turn right on Bridge St.
Sutter Buttes
Butte slough Rd. ↑
COLUSA ■
5.7
45
20
Meridian Rd.
3.6
Mawson Rd.
Pass Road
views of the Buttes
MERIDIAN ■
to YUBA CITY
20
4
So. Drexler Rd.
Moroni Rd.
Meridian Road
Garmire Road
watch for left turn on Meridian
5.2
go left on Meridian
Sacramento River
Acme Rd.
Tisdale Rd.
Coles Rd.
Knights Landing to Princeton 59.3 miles
Cranmore Road
Pelger Rd.
24.5
45
Subaco Rd.
Kirkville Rd.
Seymour Rd.
to WILLIAMS →
Cranmore Road
to YUBA CITY
5
note: turn left on Cranmore Rd. just after crossing the drawbridge
Cranmore Road
KNIGHTS LANDING
113
E10
9
Road 13
.8
113
E8
to WOODLAND 8.5 ↓
Rd. 102
8.5
↓ to 5
8.5

Crossing the Sacramento River at Princeton, Colusa County

Knights Landing to
Princeton Ferry along
the Sacramento River

Knights Landing, where scenes
were filmed around 1929 for
the movie SHOWBOAT, begins
this drive along the levee
roads of the Sacramento River.
Levee roads offer views of both
the river and agricultural land.
I watch tomatoes being harvested.
Occasionally, trucks would spill some at a
turn in the road and the blood-red squashed fruit looked
like a mortal wound in the pavement.
Blue and white herons watch me pass. Scores of
dragonflies dodge my car. Later I get a good view of
Sutter Buttes, the unusual little mountain range in the
center of the Sacramento Valley where John C.
Fremont camped in 1846. There are walnut and
peach orchards and more levees to ride on the
way to the Princeton Ferry.

Wheatland to Smartville

Annual grasses make up much of the vegetation in this rolling Sierra foothill country. The road passes through the Spenceville Wildlife Area, most glorious when clad in the green of spring.

Classic groves of blue, live, and valley oaks decorate the hillsides. Seated among old headstones in a hillside cemetery on McGanny Lane, I draw a view of the hamlet of Smartville. It is at Smartville that I begin to feel the atmosphere of California's gold country. The 1870 church is still the most prominent building in town and at the top of O'Brien Street is the old frame Masonic Temple.

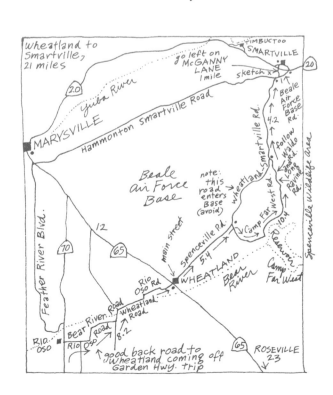

Wheatland to Smartville, 21 miles

go left on McGANNY LANE 1 mile

TIMBUCTOO SMARTVILLE

sketch x

20

Beale Air Force Base Rd.

4.2

follow Waldo Loma Rica Long Ravine Rd.

Spenceville Wildlife Area

20

Yuba River

MARYSVILLE

Hammonton Smartville Road

Wheatland-Smartville Rd.

Beale Air Force Base

note: this road enters Base (avoid)

Camp Far West Rd.

10.4

Reservoir

Feather River Blvd.

12

main street

Spenceville Rd.

5.4

Camp Far West

70

65

WHEATLAND

Bear River

Rio Oso Rd.

Bear River Road

Wheatland Road

8.2

RIO OSO

Rio Oso Road

good back road to Wheatland coming off Garden Hwy. trip

65

ROSEVILLE 23

View of Smartville, Yuba County

110

Roundabout to Nevada City

Bitney Springs Road winds through the hills above the active, growing town of Grass Valley. At Bridgeport is the longest covered bridge (233 feet) in America. It spans the South Fork of the Yuba River. In 1862, when the bridge was erected, Bridgeport was a prosperous river mining town.

At French Corral I sketch the old 1850 Wells Fargo Express Office. Today a lone goat grazes alongside the iron-doored, shuttered office that once guarded millions of dollars in gold.

FRENCH CORRAL

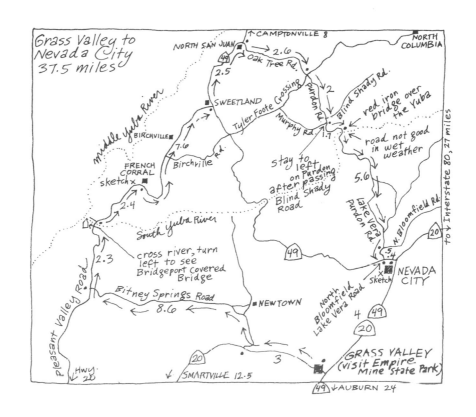

Grass Valley to
Nevada City
37.5 miles

↑CAMPTONVILLE 8
NORTH COLUMBIA
NORTH SAN JUAN
→ 2.6
Oak Tree Rd.
49
2.5
SWEETLAND
Tyler Foote Crossing
Purdon Rd.
↓ 2
Blind Shady Rd.
red iron bridge over the Yuba
Middle Yuba River
BIRCHVILLE
7.6
Birchville Rd.
Murphy Rd.
1.7
road not good in wet weather
FRENCH CORRAL
sketch x
stay to left on Purdon after passing Blind Shady Road
5.6
Lake Vera Purdon Rd.
to ↓ Interstate 80, 27 miles
2.4
South Yuba River
N. Bloomfield Rd.
cross river, turn left to see Bridgeport Covered Bridge
49
.5
20
2.3
sketch
NEVADA CITY
Pleasant Valley Road
Bitney Springs Road
8.6
NEWTOWN
North Bloomfield Lake Vera Road
4
49
20
↓ Hwy 20
↓ SMARTVILLE 12.5
20
3
GRASS VALLEY (visit Empire Mine State Park)
49 ↓AUBURN 24

The first settler here was, as you might suppose, a
Frenchman who built a corral for his mules in 1849.
There is little left to suggest the large, active
mining community that grew here soon after
the discovery of gold in the area.
    The road to Purdon Crossing over the South
Yuba River wouldn't be one to take in wet
weather. I travel it at 10 miles per hour
    and cross the boulder-strewn Yuba on an
    old, but decorative, red iron bridge.

FOR SALE
1 GOAT MILKING NUBIAN $75
WINCH TRUCK $200
WELDING TANKS. ETC. $225
10 KW GENERATOR SAS 110-220 MOBIL UNIT $1500

French Corral, Nevada County

In Nevada City there is much
to draw of historical interest.
I choose to draw the more than
100-year-old Mulloy house. It
still stands proudly at the
head of — and as you will
discover — in the middle of
Broad Street. Mulloy
had been part owner
of the Nevada
Gazette, as well as
a grocer, a
Justice of the
Peace, and a
county supervisor.

The house on Broad Street,
Nevada City, Nevada County

Nevada City to North Bloomfield and Washington

At Malakoff Diggins, before reaching North Bloomfield, I view the multicolored, pinnacled minarets of earth left by man's attempt to wash away mountains for gold. In the 1870s hydraulic mining was used to find gold that panning, cradles, and long toms couldn't uncover.

Malakoff Diggins, Nevada County

Farmers objected to all the debris carried downstream by the ruthless procedure, and in 1884 — in a court case that received wide attention — Judge Lorenzo Sawyer handed down a ruling that would control future hydraulic mining in California. Millions of dollars in gold undoubtedly still lie in those mountains.

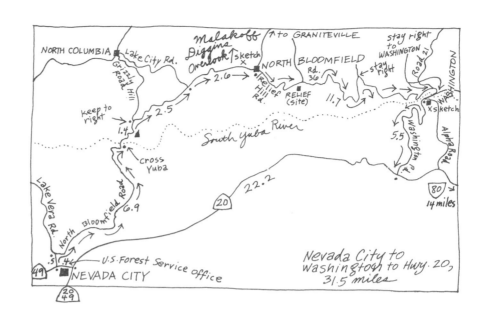

NORTH COLUMBIA Lake City Rd. *Malakoff* ↑ to GRANITEVILLE stay right to WASHINGTON
Diggins Overlook ↑ sketch NORTH BLOOMFIELD Road 21
Grizzly Road Hill × sketch 2.6 NORTH BLOOMFIELD Rd. 36 stay right
keep to right 2.5 Relief Hill Rd. RELIEF (site) 11.7 stay right WASHINGTON
1.4 cross Yuba South Yuba River × sketch
Lake Vera Rd. 5.5 Washington Rd. Alpha Road
North Bloomfield Road 6.9 22.2 20 80 14 miles
.5 .46 U.S. Forest Service office
49 NEVADA CITY
20 49

Nevada City to Washington to Hwy. 20, 31.5 miles

North Bloomfield is a shaded community of old, well-kept houses and historic buildings, maintained by the Park Service. At Washington I sketch the general store. I notice three small hotels here and a restaurant, and I learn that the siren atop the general store goes off on Mondays at noon (unless the siren person forgets).

FIRE

FAIR

General store, Washington, Nevada County

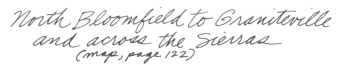

North Bloomfield to Graniteville
and across the Sierras
(map, page 122)

Graniteville, at 4,900 feet elevation,
is in the High Sierras. Gold was
mined in gulches here as far back
as 1850, but after 1883 its
existence depended on quartz
mining and lumbering. Today it
is a peaceful community where
residents appreciate a quiet and
simple life in a remote and
beautiful place. I stop to draw
and to talk to the owners of the
1859 house that had been the
residence of the local judge.

A cedar and a ponderosa pine,
planted in front in 1895, have since
grown to dwarf the old house.
Very few trees were here at
that time because the lumber of the
area had been used up for housing
and mine timber.

The only road going east out
of Graniteville takes me to
Bowman Lake, Jackson Meadow
Reservoir, and, finally, to
Highway 89. I realize I have
crossed the mighty Sierras
on a back road!

The Judge's Place, Graniteville, Nevada County

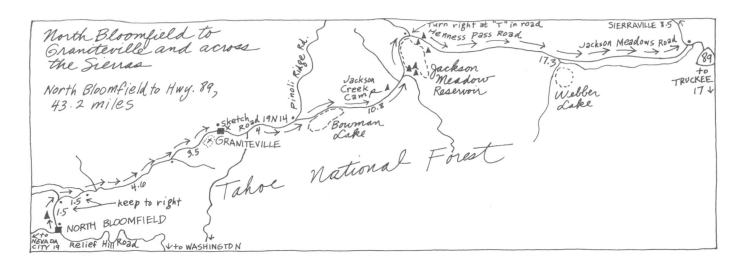

North Bloomfield to Graniteville and across the Sierras

North Bloomfield to Hwy. 89, 43.2 miles

(map labels:) Turn right at "T" in road "Henness Pass Road" · SIERRAVILLE 8.5 · Jackson Meadows Road · 89 to TRUCKEE 17 ↓ · 17.3 · Webber Lake · Pinoli Ridge Rd. · Jackson Meadow Reservoir · Jackson Creek Camp · 10.8 · Sketch Road 19N14 · 4 · GRANITEVILLE · Bowman Lake · 3.5 · Tahoe National Forest · 4.6 · 1.5 keep to right · 1.5 · NORTH BLOOMFIELD · ← to NEVADA CITY 19 · Relief Hill Road · ↓ to WASHINGTON

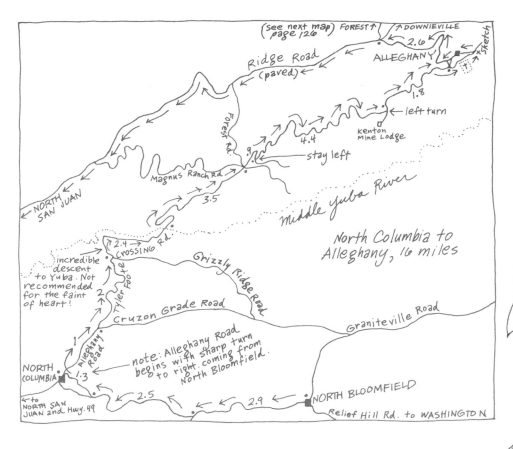

(map labels:) (see next map page 126) FOREST ↑ ↑ DOWNIEVILLE · 2.6 · ALLEGHANY · T · Sketch · Ridge Road (paved) · 1.8 · left turn · Forest Rd. · Kenton Mine Lodge · 4.4 · .9 stay left · Magnus Ranch Rd. · Middle Yuba River · NORTH SAN JUAN · 3.5 · North Columbia to Alleghany, 16 miles · 2.4 Crossing Rd. · incredible descent to Yuba. Not recommended for the faint of heart! · 2 · Tyler Foote · Grizzly Ridge Road · Cruzon Grade Road · Graniteville Road · 1 · Alleghany Road · note: Alleghany Road begins with sharp turn to right coming from North Bloomfield. · NORTH COLUMBIA · 1.3 · 2.5 · 2.9 · NORTH BLOOMFIELD · Relief Hill Rd. to WASHINGTON · ← to NORTH SAN JUAN and Hwy. 49

North Columbia to Alleghany back road

I pick the old A.D. Foote toll road to reach Alleghany. It seems incredible that men would build such a road, hewn out of rock and threading its way along a nearly perpendicular canyon wall. At several turns, walls of dry masonry are observed supporting sections of precipitous roadway.

At the beginning of the journey it is somewhat intimidating to find a sign, "Narrow road, no turnouts, one lane, last turn around." I make it, however, sometimes at a bumpy 5 miles per hour. I ford the Yuba at Footes Crossing, drive on for big views of canyons and mountains, and eventually reach the high Sierra town of Alleghany. It is strung out along the mountainside in picturesque fashion. I sit to draw the tiny building that housed the town's fire department. (A new building has since been built.) This colorful town of shiny, sloping metal roofs was established in the 1850s and is one of the few working gold-mining communities in the area.

From here it is easy to return to Highway 49, for the road is paved and there are more good views of forests and mountains to enjoy.

This is the old Henness Pass Road, the main emigrant trail, established in 1859, from Virginia City, Nevada, to Marysville.

ALLEGHANY USPS FIRE TOOL CACHE

NO PARKING ANY TIME

ALLEGHANY FIRE DEPT

Old Alleghany Fire Department building

Alleghany to Forest, Camptonville or Downieville

In the middle 1850s Forest was a lively mining camp. When it became a town it was named for a Mrs. Mooney, a newspaperwoman with the unlikely first name of Forest. She signed her journalistic efforts, "Forest City."

I arrive in Forest to find a small, quiet alpine community. Opposite the Ruby Mine Office, I sit under an apple tree and sketch. When I first visited Forest it housed the operators of nearby gold mines. Today that particular operation has ceased—although there is still interest in local mines. Behind the office, in the gully, is the entrance to a caved-in mining tunnel. When miles of tunnels were being used here, one could go all the way to Alleghany without caring about winter snow. Forest and Alleghany were connected by all the mining tunnels!

RUBY MINE
OFFICE

House at Forest, Sierra County

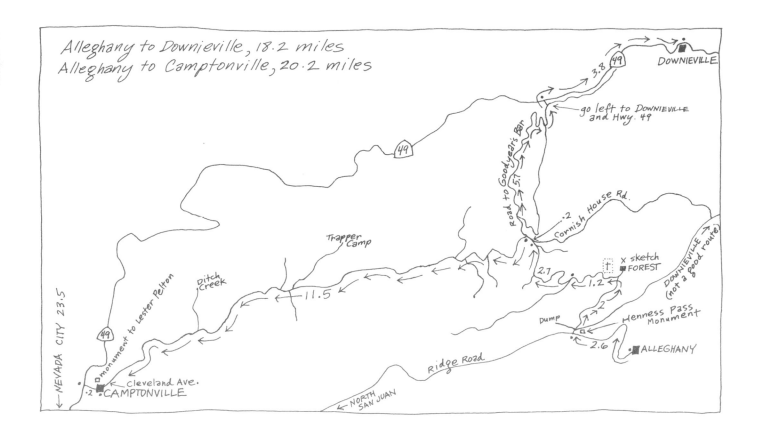

I then travel to the charming, historic town of Downieville via Goodyear's Bar, a winding mountain road, narrow, steep, and rough. I get a strong impression of the tremendous dimension and depth of these canyons of the High Sierras.

An easier route, yet with grand mountain views, is the road to Camptonville. Named for a blacksmith, Robert Campton, the little town is noted as the place where Lester Pelton invented the Pelton Water Wheel in 1878.

Back road, Mourning Dove,
Sierra County

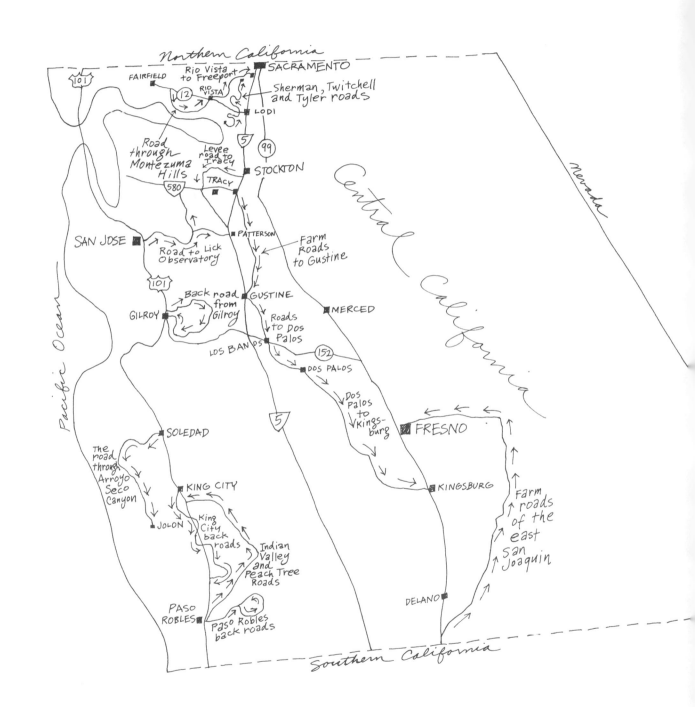

Northern California

101
FAIRFIELD
Rio Vista to Freeport
SACRAMENTO
12
RIO VISTA
Sherman, Twitchell and Tyler roads
LODI
Road through Montezuma Hills
Levee road to Tracy
5
99
STOCKTON
580
TRACY
PATTERSON
SAN JOSE
Road to Lick Observatory
Farm Roads to Gustine
Central California
Nevada
101
Back road from Gilroy
GUSTINE
MERCED
GILROY
Roads to Dos Palos
LOS BANOS
152
DOS PALOS
Dos Palos to Kingsburg
5
SOLEDAD
FRESNO
The road through Arroyo Seco Canyon
KING CITY
KINGSBURG
Farm roads of the east san Joaquin
JOLON
King City back roads
Indian Valley and Peach Tree Roads
PASO ROBLES
Paso Robles back roads
DELANO
Pacific Ocean
Southern California

128

Eucalyptus, Santa Cruz County

Central California

With some good maps and an extra bit of time,
I set off — still with a sense of adventure
in taking a back route and coming upon
the unexpected.
I believe we all need to express
our appreciation of beauty. What better
way to fulfill this need than by
getting closer to nature on the
back roads.

The road through Montezuma Hills (map, page 133)

Along Shiloh Road the land is rolling. Occasional eucalyptus trees bend in the wind. I pass through Birds Landing, a shipping point for hay and wheat in the 1870s. The old Benjamin Store (1875) still stands. Almost forgotten, Collinsville hamlet slumbers at the river's edge, where the San Joaquin joins the Sacramento. The handsome profile of Mount Diablo is outlined across the water. Long ago Collinsville was a salmon fishing village. The many fishermen from Italy who worked in the cannery lived in houses built on stilts to allow flood tides to pass beneath. The town was referred to as "Little Venice."

Farm near Birds Landing, Solano County

Cows, sheep, flocks of crows, hawks, lonely farms,
and lonelier windmills are seen while driving through
the Montezuma Hills from Birds Landing.
   The road to Rio Vista curves among the summer
golden hills of Montezuma.

In town, at the corner of California and 4th streets, I draw St. Joseph's Church, built in 1904. The style of this all-wood structure is Carpenter's Gothic, and its stained glass windows are quite wonderful.

St. Joseph's Church, Rio Vista, Solano County

Sherman, Brannan, Twitchell, and Tyler

There are meandering levee roads off Highway 160 beginning with Sherman Island Road, which follows the broad San Joaquin River, then Three Mile Slough. Brannan Island Road and Twitchell Island Road bring views of corn, grain, and hay crops on the land side, boats, wind surfers and skiers on the water side.

Fairfield to Collinsville to Rio Vista, 37.9 miles
Antioch to Walnut Grove on delta island back roads, 46.1 miles
Rio Vista to Freeport, 30.4 miles

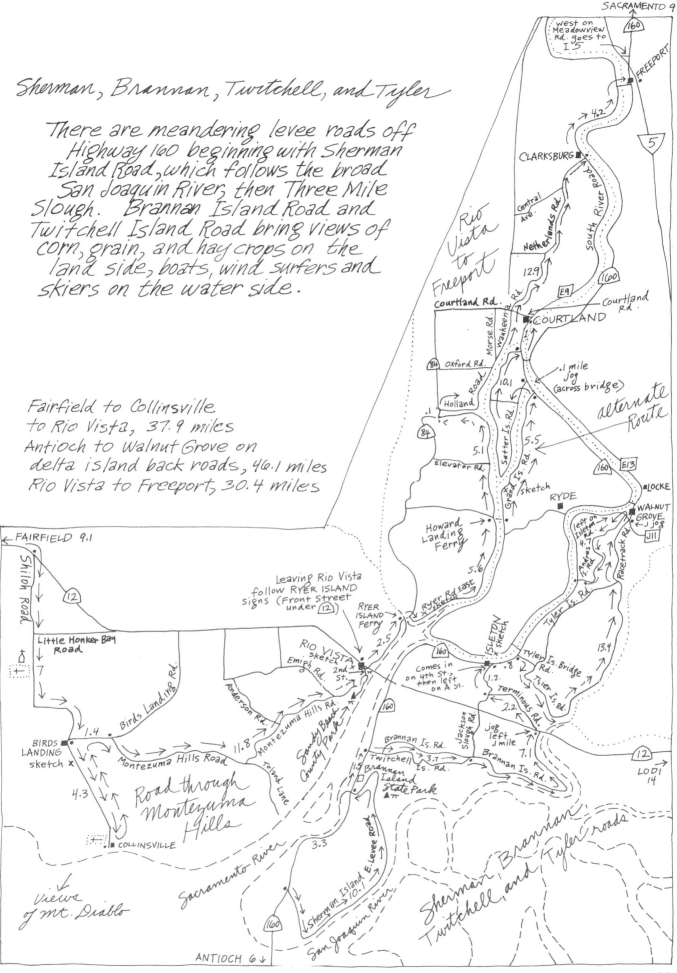

Old City Hall, Isleton, Solano County

The towering dredge moored at Isleton is the town's most prominent feature. I sketch the City Hall, which during my visit was still in use. Unfortunately, the 1989 earthquake caused severe structural damage to this historic 1920s building. I complete my meandering with a drive around Tyler Island which brings me again to Highway 160.

Rio Vista to Clarksburg and Freeport (map, page 133)

I find Rio Vista a clean, pleasant riverside town. An attractive marina is nearby and a county park for camping and picnicking along the Sacramento River. The area is now the 5th-ranked wind surfing spot worldwide.

I stopped to see the Dutra Museum of Dredging. The Dutra family have made their lovely 1907 house into a comprehensive and significant presentation of the history of dredging in the Delta region.

I sketch a huge bucket used on the dredge Tule King, constructed in 1910. Its 25,000 pounds tower over the family cat in the Dutra backyard. Phone 707-374-5701 for an appointment to see the museum.

Tule King dredge bucket, Rio Vista, Solano County

Going north I ride the free ferry
to Ryer Island and sketch a well-proportioned
sailboat docked in Hidden Harbor.
     The day is quiet and bird sounds predominate.
Geese pose in the water. A commercial crayfisher-
man speaks to me. His 150 traps are inspected
daily in the warm summer months. One sardine and a
can of dogfood are used as bait in each trap. His
take in one trap can be anywhere from one to one
hundred crayfish. Once hauled in, the crayfish
are frozen and shipped to Sweden, where they
are most particularly relished.

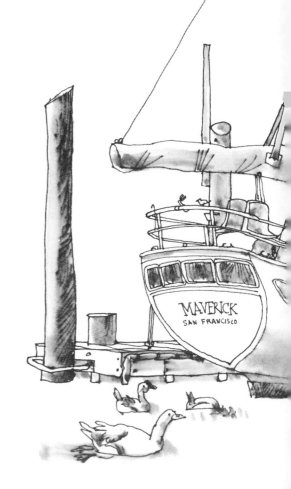

Delta boat, Ryer Island, Sacramento County

137

An alternate route, Rio Vista to Courtland and Freeport
(map, page 133)

This road differs from the previous road in that a second free ferry at Howard Landing takes you onto Grand Island, then north again toward Freeport. Along this route, Sutter Island and Merritt Island are also traversed. On Grand Island I draw a fine Victorian house along Steamboat Slough.

House on Steamboat Slough, Yolo County

I ride the levees, eventually arriving in Freeport, once a major shipping center for the gold mines. A·J·Bump built the first general store/saloon in town in 1863. It is still there when I arrive on a warm summer day in July; a cool drink at the colorful, old saloon tastes good. (map, page 133)

Levee road to Tracy

Strange as it seems, there are numerous islands right in the center of California. Flood plains of the Sacramento and San Joaquin rivers, reclaimed over the years for agriculture, created the many islands.

Riding levee roads requires a sharp eye all around. The levees give a command position for appreciating the waterways and the special look of island agriculture.

I sketch a historic country schoolhouse off Inland Road. It was built in 1904 and abandoned in 1946.

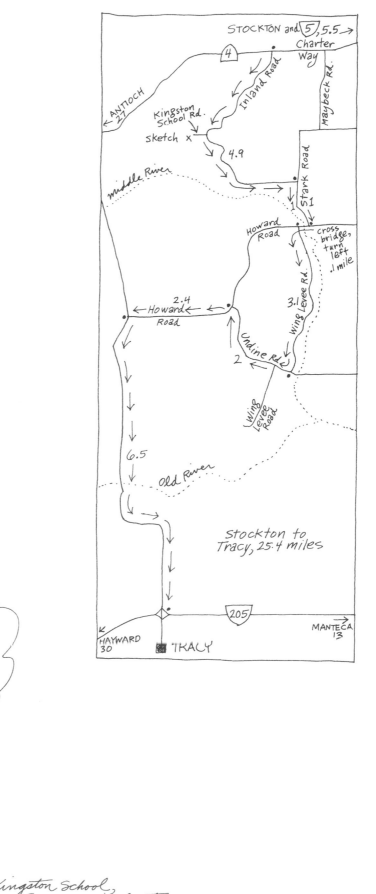

STOCKTON and 5, 5.5 →
4
Charter Way
ANTIOCH 27
Inland Road
Maybeck Rd.
Kingston School Rd.
sketch x
4.9
middle River
Stark Road
1 .1
Howard Road
cross bridge, turn left .1 mile
Wing Levee Rd.
2.4 ← Howard ← Road
3.1
Undine Rd.
2 ←
Wing Levee Road
6.5
Old River
Stockton to Tracy, 25.4 miles
205
K HAYWARD 30
TRACY
MANTECA 13

Kingston School,
San Joaquin County

The road
to Lick
Observatory
and San Antonio
Valley

It is a windy day and overcast with thick, dark clouds.
The still green hills have begun to turn brown in some
areas. Wildflowers are cheerful spots of color on this
gray day. I stop to draw a view of Lick Observatory—
framed with oaks—visible along the ridge of Mount
Hamilton. As I drive the winding road, ground squirrels
scurry back and forth to their burrows in the bases of
ancient oak trees. You can see the mighty 120"
telescope any day of the week.

Lick Observatory, Mount Hamilton, Santa Clara County

It is 50 miles from here to Livermore on Lick Observatory Road, which winds down the east side of Mount Hamilton and through the lovely oak meadows of San Antonio Valley. Here the road divides, going north to Livermore and east to Patterson.

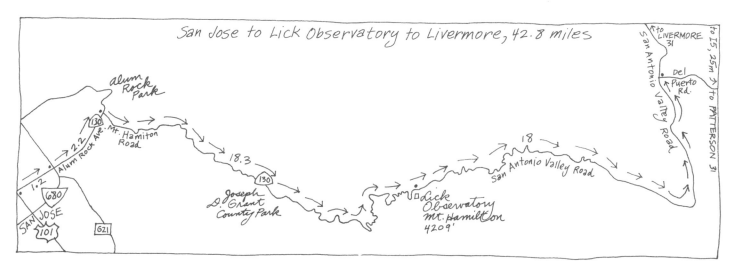

San Jose to Lick Observatory to Livermore, 42.8 miles

Back road from Gilroy

The town of Gilroy was named
for John Gilroy, soapmaker and
millwright. He had married the
daughter of Ygnacio Ortega, owner
of Rancho San Ysidro, and was given part
of the Rancho (4,460 acres) when Ygnacio
died in 1833.

La Canada Ranch, near Gilroy,
Santa Clara County

145

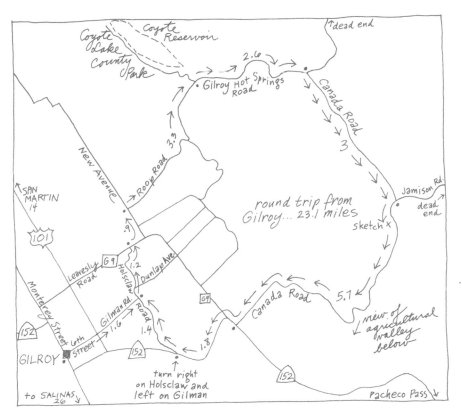

Back road mailbox

John was influential enough for the present town
of Gilroy to be named for him; however, in 1869 he died
in poverty, aged 73 years. It is interesting that his
name was really Cameron. Gilroy was his mother's
maiden name, which he took when he deserted
ship at Monterey in 1814 so as not to be traced.
    I sketch a scene along Canada Road, a ranch
nestled at the base of sloping hills. Poppies, mustard,
and purple vetch bloom on this bright spring day.
    I watch a bobcat warily cross the road
and bound through grass and flowers.

The road through Arroyo Seco Canyon

I see the harvesting of lettuce on my way. A huge motorized sprinkler creeps over the planted landscape of cabbage, onions, and grape crops! One large unplanted field is orange with poppies.

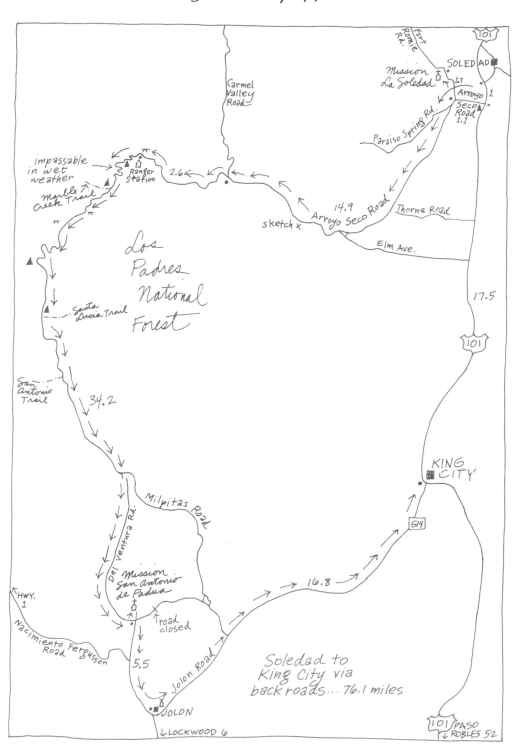

I draw a white barn and the complex canyon walls of Arroyo Seco, while the ranch dog returns a large rock for me to throw again and again.

Gould Ranch, Arroyo Seco Canyon, Monterey County

It is April, and with forest fires unlikely and the temperature comfortable, an ideal time to travel this colorful road. The road ends at Mission San Antonio de Padua, founded in 1771 and one of the most picturesque of the California missions. It stands in the valley of the San Antonio River and had been well known for its high quality wheat and fine horses.

The road narrows in Los Padres National Forest and winds along mountain ledges. Yucca blooms in creamy white splendor, and firewood, ceanothus, monkey flower, paintbrush, and yerba santa color the roadside.

Grapevine in May, near King City,
Monterey County

King City back roads

On Oasis Road I see thousands of grapevines patterning the hills and dales south of King City. They are all marked, cordoned, and prepared for mechanical harvesting. I draw an Early Burgundy varietal at the flowering stage when young grape bunches are just beginning. A sprinkling device is attached to this grape stake. An airplane is dusting other vineyards in the vicinity with sulphur, but I am lucky to be distant enough from this activity.

The roads parallel Highway 101 and I find myself south of San Ardo surrounded by a forest of oil pump jacks. I hold my nose and clear this area as I proceed inland on Sargeants Valley Road. Brown rolling hills and golden grain fields fill the landscape.

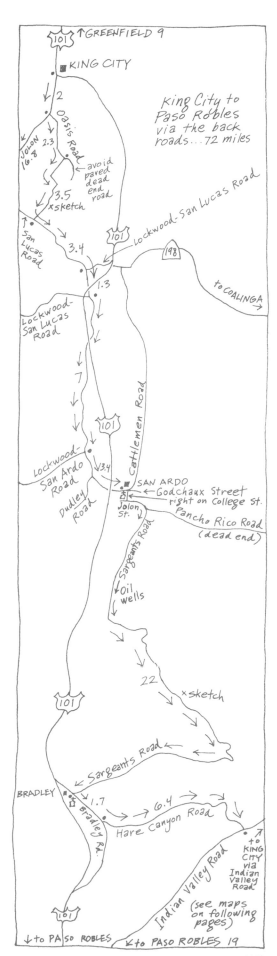

King City to Paso Robles via the back roads... 72 miles

101 ↑GREENFIELD 9
■KING CITY
↓ 2
Oasis Road
JOLON 16.8
avoid paved dead end road
↓3.5 ×sketch
↑San Lucas Road
3.4
101
Lockwood-San Lucas Road
198
to COALINGA
1.3
Lockwood-San Lucas Road
↓7
101
Cattlemen Road
Lockwood-San Ardo Road
↓3.4
Dudley Road
■SAN ARDO
←Godchaux Street
right on College St.
Jolon St.
Pancho Rico Road (dead end)
Sargeants Road
↓Oil wells
22 ×sketch
Sargeants Road
101
BRADLEY
↓1.7
Bradley Rd.
6.4
Hare Canyon Road
Indian Valley Road
↑to KING CITY via Indian Valley Road
(see maps on following pages)
101
↓to PASO ROBLES   ↓to PASO ROBLES 19

I stop to draw a Pinto horse—
an inspired design for a
mailbox made of welded steel
parts.   You can return to
Highway 101 at Bradley or
take Hare Canyon Road
and Indian Valley Road to
King City or Paso Robles.

Pinto mailbox, near Bradley, Monterey County

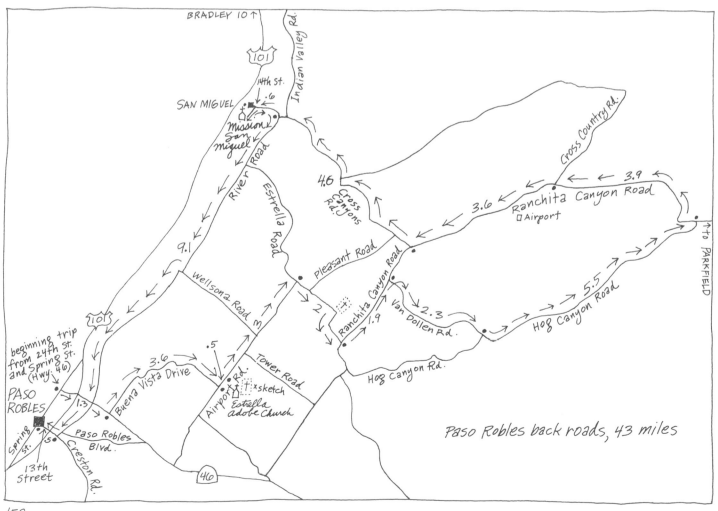

BRADLEY 10↑

101

14th St.
SAN MIGUEL   .6

Indian Valley Rd.

Mission
San
Miguel

Cross Country Rd.

River Road
Estrella Road

4.6

Cross Canyons Rd.

3.9
3.6
Ranchita Canyon Road
☐ Airport

9.1

Pleasant Road

Wellsona Road

Ranchita Canyon Road

2

↑ to PARKFIELD

5.5
Hog Canyon Road

1.9
Van Dollen Rd.
2.3

3

beginning trip
from 24th St.
and Spring St.
(Hwy. 46)

101

Hog Canyon Rd.

PASO
ROBLES

1.3

.5

3.6

Buena Vista Drive

Airport Rd.

Tower Road

×sketch

Estrella
adobe Church

Paso Robles back roads, 43 miles

Spring St.

.5

Paso Robles
Blvd.

13th
Street

Creston Rd.

46

Paso Robles back roads

On the plains of Estrella, in 1879, Christian pioneers built Estrella Adobe Church. It was restored in 1952 and part of the cemetery was saved. From the grave markers, I am able to piece together the heart-tugging story of the Stovall family: Little Albert, the youngest, whose headstone reads "Born May 13, 1881, son died May 4, 1885

Twas our laughing blue eyed Boy
Our comfort and our household joy
Over the river he beckons to me
The gates of the city we
        cannot see";
then the middle son Walter M. (September 8, 1875 – May 23, 1885); mother Mary C. (died March 15, 1905, 63 years 18 days); and father F.M. (died August 16, 1907, 64 years /1 mo./18 dys.).

Evan P's marker is pictured here. Sentimental verse has its effect on me!

Roads wind around here and over rolling hills textured with grain, hay crops, and vineyards. A large hawk poses on a fencepost.

I stop to explore Mission San Miguel Archangel, a lovely old church founded in 1797, and then return to Paso Robles on River Road.

EVAN P.
SON OF
F. M. & M. C.
STOVALL
BORN
OCT. 30, 1878
DIED
JUNE 15, 1885

The angels to Evan did whisper,
Jesus has called you away,
To join your dear Brothers in Heaven
Our darling did meekly obey.

Headstone at Estrella Adobe Church graveyard, near Paso Robles, San Luis Obispo County

153

Indian Valley and Peach Tree roads

Along Indian Valley and Peach Tree roads, I see pleasant vistas aplenty of valleys, farms, rolling hills, majestic oaks, and pines. Shaded by a giant oak, I sketch a view of Peach Tree and Hidalgo canyons looking west into the late afternoon sun.

On Freeman Flat Road vineyards create a rolling sea of row upon row of intensely green vines.

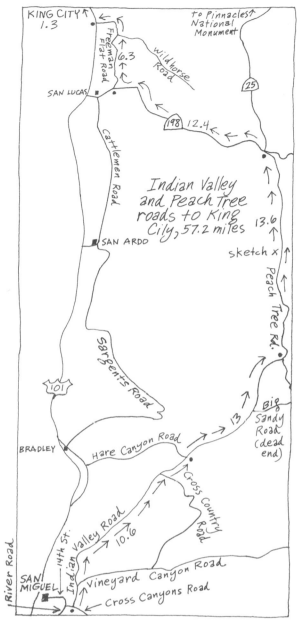

Indian Valley and Peach Tree roads to King City, 57.2 miles

KING CITY 1.3
to Pinnacles National Monument
Freeman Flat Road
6.3
Wildhorse Road
SAN LUCAS
25
198 12.4
sketch x
13.6
Peach Tree Rd.
Cattlemen Road
SAN ARDO
Sargents Road
101
Big Sandy Road (dead end)
13
BRADLEY
Hare Canyon Road
Cross Country Road
Indian Valley Road
10.6
River Road
14th St.
SAN MIGUEL
Vineyard Canyon Road
Cross Canyons Road

Peach Tree Canyon, Monterey County

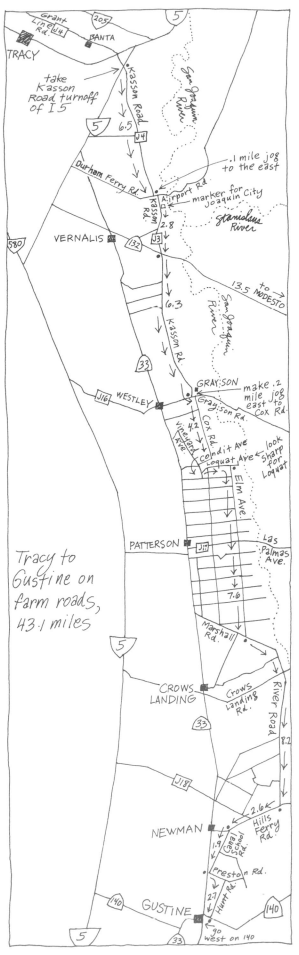

Farm roads through the San Joaquin Valley

From Tracy palm-lined Kasson Road goes south, beginning a farm road journey directly through California's greatest agricultural valley. On a clear day the snow-capped Sierras can be viewed to the east. I stop to read a marker at the site of San Joaquin City, established in 1849. In 1880 it had a hotel, warehouse, two saloons, stores, and houses. Pioneers and freight wagons crossed the river at nearby Durham Ferry. The Spanish explorer Gabriel Moraga had named this river San Joaquin in 1813.

Later, I drive around the village of Grayson, noting the many little churches. Along Elm Road I pass a unique enterprise, a turf farm.

In the pleasant town of Gustine, I sketch a small grove of orange trees along its main thoroughfare. Gustine's old-fashioned water tower is in the background. Sighting the water tower is often the first indication of a town in the offing as these farm roads proceed.

Orange trees, Gustine, Merced County

Roads to San Luis Camp and Dos Palos (map, page 160)

A short diversion onto Mercey Springs and Wolfsen roads brings me to San Luis Camp adobe, the oldest building in the county. It was built in 1848 by Francisco Pacheco and became a stopping place for vaqueros driving cattle to the gold fields. When land baron Henry Miller was in the area, he usually stayed here.

Further on I travel through the San Luis Wildlife Refuge. There is a herd of Tule elk in a large enclosure, where one massive-horned bull elk has corralled all the females. Other bulls stand a long way off, quite deserted and forlorn looking. Some 800 Tule elk are all that remain of the 500,000 that once roamed the grasslands of the San Joaquin Valley. Many ducks, eagles, hawks, and heron are also to be seen in the refuge.

San Luis Camp adobe, Merced County

159

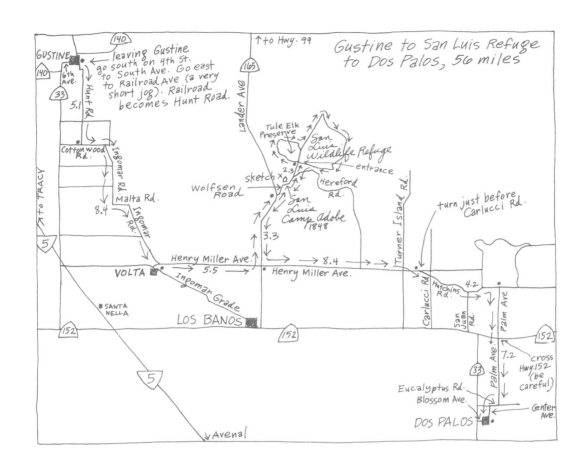

140

GUSTINE

↑to Hwy. 99

165

leaving Gustine
go south on 4th St.
South Ave. Go east
to Railroad Ave (a very
short jog). Railroad
becomes Hunt Road.

140

6th Ave.

33

Hunt Rd.

5.1

Lander Ave

Tule Elk Preserve

San Luis Wildlife Refuge

entrance

Cottonwood Rd.

Ingomar Rd.

sketch X

2.3

Wolfsen Road

Hereford Rd.

→ to TRACY

Malta Rd.

8.4

Ingomar Rd.

San Luis Camp Adobe 1848

Turner Island Rd.

turn just before Carlucci Rd.

3.3

5

Henry Miller Ave.

5.5

→ 8.4 →

Henry Miller Ave.

VOLTA

Ingomar Grade

Henry Miller Ave.

Carlucci Rd.

Hutchins Rd.

4.2

Palm Ave

SANTA NELLA

152

LOS BANOS

152

152

5

San Juan Rd.

cross Hwy. 152 (be careful)

33

Palm Ave

7.2

↓ Avenal

Eucalyptus Rd.
Blossom Ave.

DOS PALOS

Center Ave.

Dos Palos to Kingsburg

In a small brochure called "The
Fertile Fields of Dos Palos Colony,"
published in 1902, farmers were
coaxed by landowners Miller and
Lux to buy and settle here. Land was
$30 to $75 per acre at 6% interest.

Beekeepers realized
that in Dos Palos
(Two Poles) the rich
alfalfa crop aided in
creating the thickest,
richest, whitest honey
in the world. 60,000
dozen eggs a year were
produced, alfalfa sold
f.o.b. at $8.50 per ton,
cows sold for $45 to $60
a head.

Water tower of Dos Palos, Merced County

Two passenger trains as well as two freight trains ran every day to San Francisco, making daily newspapers available. Today Dos Palos continues as a booming agricultural town, center for a large area of diversified farming.

I sketch the water tower, though it is not as quaint as Gustine's.

On my trip south I see farm roads lined with wads of cotton blown from truck trailers during harvest time. Big red corn harvesters gather in a winter crop of dried corn and process it; the kernels are then loaded into trucks and carted away.

Nearing Kingsburg, I sketch in the cemetery I remember from my youth, where my mother, dad, and grandparents are buried. It is still a meticulously well-kept place. The cypress trees are even taller than I remember.

Kingsburg itself is a fine valley town with a Swedish theme to its main street (Draper Street) architecture. Reaching Kingsburg, I have now traversed a good part of the San Joaquin Valley on farm roads.

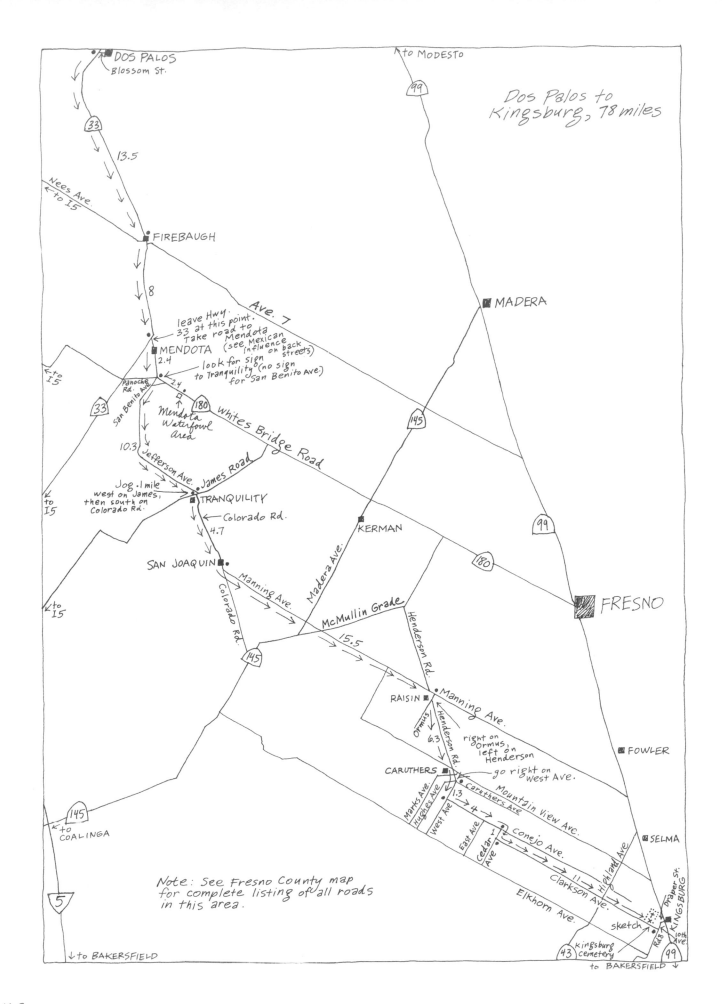

DOS PALOS
Blossom St.

to MODESTO

99

Dos Palos to
Kingsburg, 78 miles

33

13.5

Nees Ave.
to I5

FIREBAUGH

MADERA

8

Ave. 7

leave Hwy.
33 at this point.
Take road to Mendota
Mendota (see Mexican
influence on back
streets)

MENDOTA
2.4

look for sign
to Tranquility (no sign
for San Benito Ave.)

to
I5

Panoche Rd.
2.4

180

145

33

San Benito Ave.

Whites Bridge Road

Mendota
Waterfowl
area

10.3

Jefferson Ave.

James Road

to
I5

99

Jog .1 mile
west on James,
then south on
Colorado Rd.

TRANQUILITY

Colorado Rd.

180

KERMAN

4.7

SAN JOAQUIN

Colorado Rd.

Manning Ave.

Madera Ave.

to
I5

McMullin Grade

FRESNO

15.5

Henderson Rd.

145

Manning Ave.

RAISIN

Ormus

Henderson Rd.

6.3

right on
Ormus,
left on
Henderson

FOWLER

CARUTHERS

go right on
West Ave.

145

Marks Ave.

Hughes Ave.

1.3

Caruthers Ave.

Mountain View Ave.

to
COALINGA

West Ave.

4

East Ave.

Cedar Ave.

1

Conejo Ave.

11

Highland Ave.

SELMA

Clarkson Ave.

Elkhorn Ave.

Draper St.

KINGSBURG

5

Note: See Fresno County map
for complete listing of all roads
in this area.

sketch

Rd 8

10th Ave.

Kingsburg
cemetery

43

99

to BAKERSFIELD

to BAKERSFIELD

Cypresses, Kingsburg, Fresno County

163

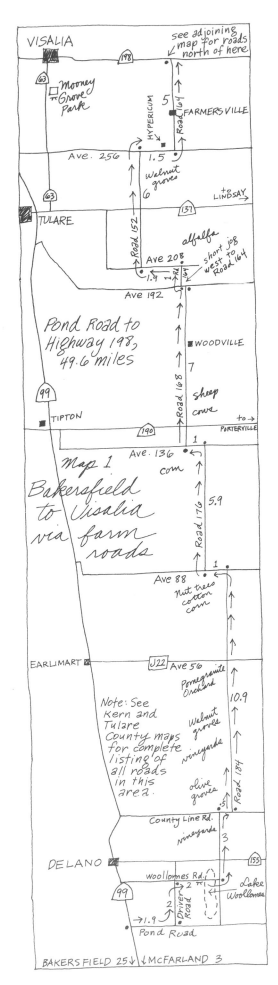

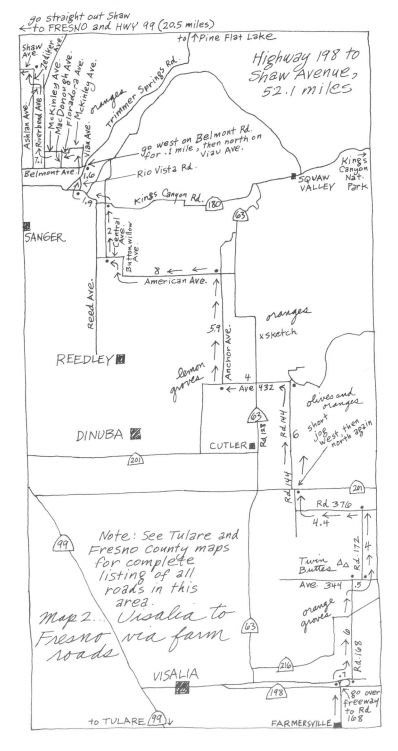

Farm roads of the east San Joaquin Valley

I turn off the busy highway and seek tranquil farm roads going north. I picnic at Lake Woollomes on the Friant Kern Canal. Driving on, I see rice and cotton crops, and olive and walnut trees, among many other vegetable and fruit crops. It is raining today and I see cows in muddy splendor near a gigantic pile of manure.

Map 1 area (left)

VISALIA
198
63
Mooney Grove Park
see adjoining map for roads north of here
HYPERICUM
5
Road 164
FARMERSVILLE
Ave. 256
1.5
Walnut groves
63
6
to LINDSAY
TULARE
137
Road 152
Ave 208
alfalfa
short jog west to Road 164
1.9
Ave 192
WOODVILLE

Pond Road to Highway 198, 49.6 miles

Road 168
7
sheep
cows
99
TIPTON
190
to PORTERVILLE
Ave. 136
1
corn

Map 1

Bakersfield to Visalia via farm roads

Road 176
5.9
Ave 88
1
Nut trees cotton corn

EARLIMART
J22
Ave 56
Pomegranite Orchard
Walnut groves
vineyards
10.9
Road 184
olive groves
.5
County Line Rd.
vineyards
3

Note: See Kern and Tulare County maps for complete listing of all roads in this area.

DELANO
155
Woollomes Rd.
2
Driver Road
Lake Woollomes
99
2
1.9
Pond Road

BAKERSFIELD 25 ↓   ↓ McFARLAND 3

Map 2 area (right)

go straight out Shaw to FRESNO and HWY 99 (20.5 miles)
to Pine Flat Lake

Highway 198 to Shaw Avenue, 52.1 miles

Shaw Ave.
Zediker Ave.
Ashlan Ave.
Riverbend Ave.
McKinley Ave.
MacDonough Ave.
Floradora Ave.
McKinley Ave.
Viau Ave.
oranges
Trimmer Springs Rd.
7.1
Belmont Ave.
1.6
go west on Belmont Rd. for .1 mile, then north on Viau Ave.
Rio Vista Rd.
King's Canyon Nat. Park
SQUAW VALLEY
1.9
Kings Canyon Rd.
180
63
SANGER
2
Central Ave.
Button willow Ave.
8
American Ave.
Reed Ave.
oranges
x sketch
5.9
Anchor Ave.
REEDLEY
lemon groves
4
Ave 432
olives and oranges
63
Rd 128
Rd 144
DINUBA
CUTLER
6
short jog west then north again
201
201
Rd 376
4.4
Rd 144
Rd 172
4
Twin Buttes
Ave. 344
.5

Note: See Tulare and Fresno County maps for complete listing of all roads in this area.

Map 2... Visalia to Fresno via farm roads

orange groves
Rd. 168
63
.7
216
VISALIA
198
go over freeway to Rd 168
to TULARE 99 ↓
FARMERSVILLE

Orange groves are
dominant as I proceed
north, skirting foothills
of the Sierra Nevada mountains.
I marvel at how attractively
nature has decorated the
lush green orchard trees
with colorful oranges.

Fresno County oranges

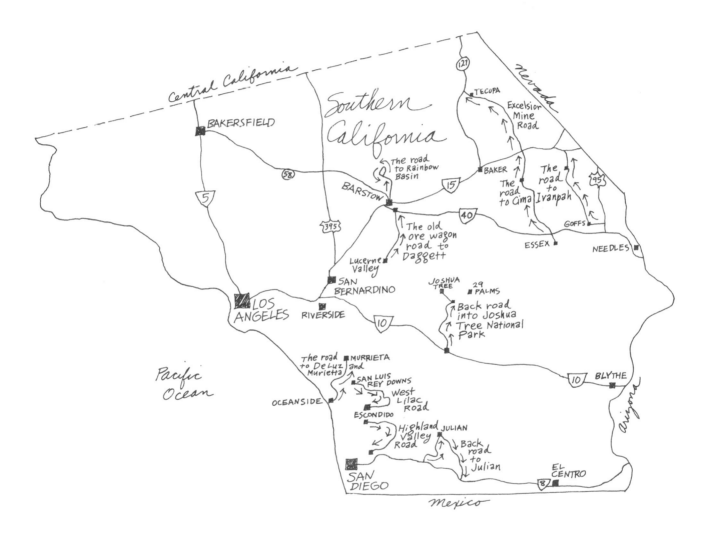

Sketching helps one to see the world through fresh eyes, to see some beauty everywhere, even where it's least expected. Henry Moore said that "one draws to concentrate knowledge." I believe that this is one of the great functions of drawing. It is a shame that more of us do not take advantage of this avenue of expression to increase our appreciation of the world.

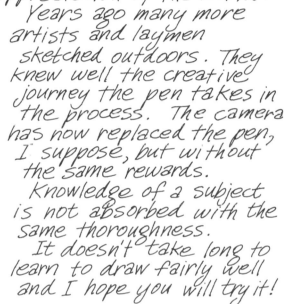

Years ago many more artists and laymen sketched outdoors. They knew well the creative journey the pen takes in the process. The camera has now replaced the pen, I suppose, but without the same rewards.

Knowledge of a subject is not absorbed with the same thoroughness.

It doesn't take long to learn to draw fairly well and I hope you will try it!

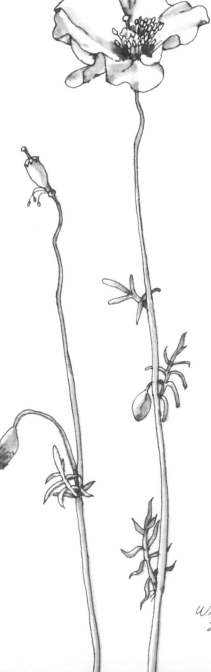

Wind Poppy,
Santa Barbara County

The road to De Luz and Murrieta

Cattle, sheep, and horses once grazed the fields in the valley where Mission San Luis Rey de Francia is located. The church was completed in 1815. Father Peyri, for 34 years the Mission's leader, was forced to leave when a law expelling all Spaniards was passed in 1829. Restoration of the Mission occurred later, and in 1893 it was rededicated as a Franciscan seminary.

Today one must drive a way to outdistance housing and shopping developments that have sprung up in the once secluded valley.

Along North River Road and Sleeping Indian Road, farming country reappears. Strawberry fields cover entire hillsides where scores of laborers pick the fruit. Plastic coverings between the plants glisten like armor plate. Other hills are textured with citrus and avocado groves.

There are palm and eucalyptus trees, and red tile-roofed houses perch on knolls in the picturesque hills.

Between De Luz and Murrieta I stop to lunch in a grove of venerable silver-barked oaks. Near Murrieta I am honored with a clear view of the snowcapped San Bernardino and San Jacinto mountains and the broad valley below.

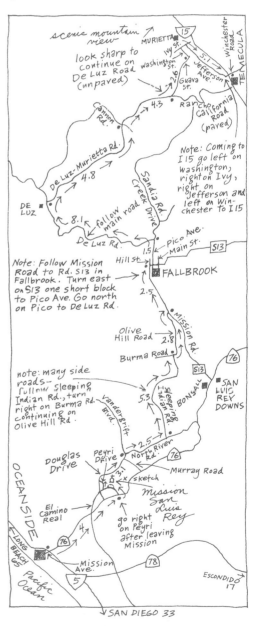

Oceanside to De Luz and Murrieta, 46.6 miles

scenic mountain view

MURIETTA

look sharp to continue on De Luz Road (unpaved)

Winchester Road

TEMECULA

Ivy St.

S.1

washington St.

Jefferson Ave.

Guava St.

2.6

Cannon Rd.

4.3

Rancho California Road (paved)

De Luz-Murrietta Rd.

4.8

Sandia Creek Drive

Note: Coming to I 15 go left on Washington, right on Ivy, right on Jefferson and left on Winchester to I 15

DE LUZ

8.1

follow main road

De Luz Rd.

1.5

Pico Ave.

Main St.

S13

Note: Follow Mission Road to Rd. S13 in Fallbrook. Turn east on S13 one short block to Pico Ave. Go north on Pico to De Luz Rd.

Hill St.

FALLBROOK

2.5

Mission Rd.

Olive Hill Road

2.8

Burma Road

S13

76

SAN LUIS REY DOWNS

note: many side roads— follow Sleeping Indian Rd., turn right on Burma Rd. continuing on Olive Hill Rd.

5.3

Sleeping Indian Rd.

BONSALL

Vandergrift Blvd.

2.5

North River Rd.

76

Douglas Drive

Peyri Drive

Murray Road

sketch

Mission San Luis Rey

El Camino Real

4

go right on Peyri after leaving Mission

OCEANSIDE

LONG BEACH 105

Pacific Ocean

76

Mission Ave.

5

78

ESCONDIDO 17

↓SAN DIEGO 33

Mission San Luis Rey, San Diego County

169

West Lilac Road

West Lilac Road runs through
up-and-down hills dotted with
avocado and citrus groves. Houses
perched here and there take advantage
of the many views of surrounding
hills and orchards. Big-leafed
avocado trees make walls of green
along the winding road. And in
other orchards, oranges and lemons
look like Christmas tree ornaments
as they ripen to full color.

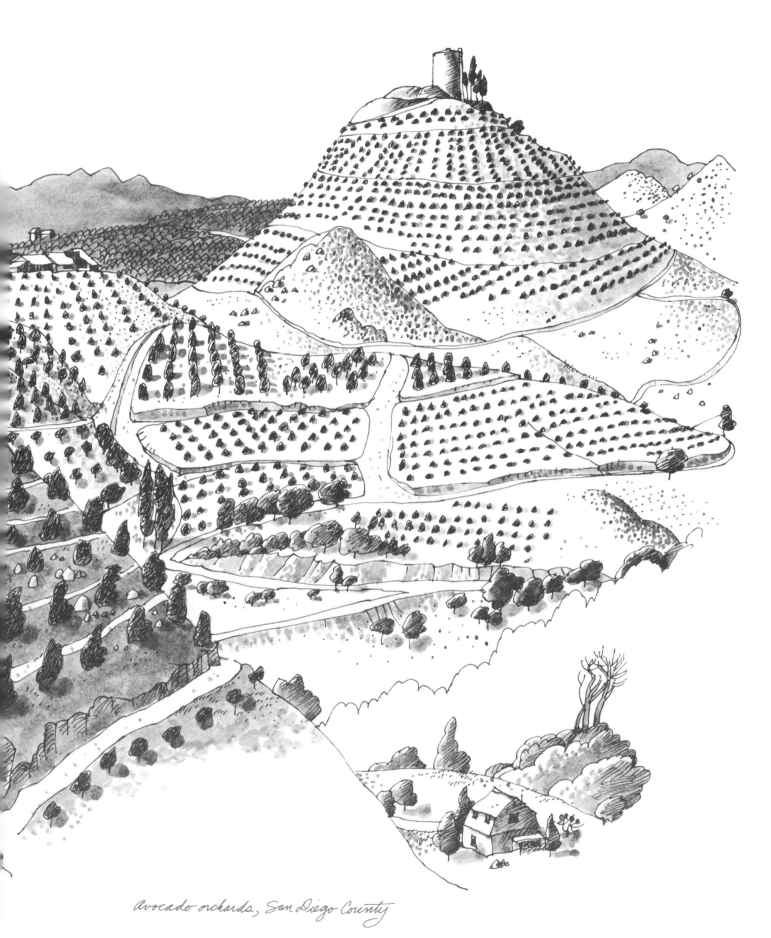

Avocado orchards, San Diego County

West Lilac Road

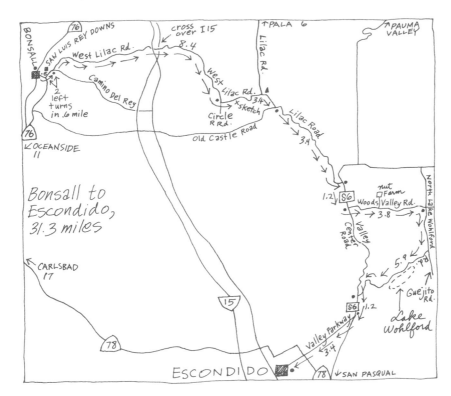

Map details:
- 76 SAN LUIS REY DOWNS
- BONSALL
- West Lilac Rd.
- cross over I15 8.4
- ↑PALA 6
- Lilac Rd.
- ↑PAUMA VALLEY
- 2 left turns in .6 mile
- Camino Del Rey
- West Lilac Rd. 3.4
- ×sketch
- Circle R Rd.
- Lilac Road 3.4
- 76
- ←OCEANSIDE 11
- Old Castle Road
- **Bonsall to Escondido, 31.3 miles**
- 1.2
- S6
- nut Farm
- Woods Valley Rd.
- 3.8
- North Lake Wohlford
- ←CARLSBAD 17
- Valley Center Road
- 5.9 .8
- Guejito Rd.
- Lake Wohlford
- 15
- S6 1.2
- Valley Parkway 3.4
- 78
- ESCONDIDO
- 78 ↓SAN PASQUAL

172

Highland Valley Road

take Highland Road exit · .3 · Highland 4 · look sharp for left turn · Highland Valley Rd. · ← Bandy Canyon Road · good views · 78 · RAMONA · 7.1 · ×sketch · Rangeland Road · Highland Valley Rd. 2.4 · Archie Moore Rd. · Pomerado Road · 67 · Warnock St. · Ramona Street · jog right on 67, then turn left on Dye Rd. .1 mile · 3 · San Vicente Rd. · 2.2 · Wildcat Canyon Road · 15 · to SAN DIEGO · 54 · POWAY · 67 · Barona Ranch Indian Reservation · Wildcat Canyon Rd. · ×sketch Barona Mission · 8.9 · Interstate 15 to Lakeside, 35.2 miles · Willow Rd. · .3 · Mapleview Rd. · LAKESIDE · EL CAJON 6 · 67

Highland Valley Road

The avocado trees in my drawing are planted strategically between colossal boulders high above San Pasqual Valley. The two elements seem to complement each other—the dark green trees and the light pink and tan rock formations.

Avocado orchard near Ramona, San Diego County

Along the mountain drive through the Barona Indian Reservation, I stop to draw the crisply white Indian Mission. The church has reddish-brown trim with Christmas lights still in place. I inspect the neat, warm interior of the little church and the pictures on the walls. It is a pleasant place indeed. Wildcat Canyon soon descends from here toward Lakeside.

Julian back road round trip

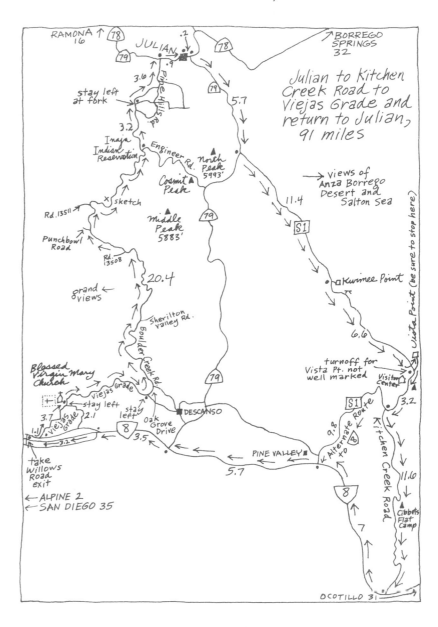

Julian to Kitchen
Creek Road to
Viejas Grade and
return to Julian,
91 miles

Barona Mission Church,
San Diego County

Julian back road round trip

A miners' rush to Julian in 1870 followed the discovery of gold in the area and lasted until about 1880. Homesteaders followed the miners, and fruit growing, bee culture, and livestock made the town a trading center. Today tourists find its historic atmosphere attractive. I begin from here and travel Highway 79 to Road S1. There are top-of-the-world views along S1 of the great and colorful Desert State Park. Row after row of beige, brown, and pink mountains fade into infinity. Later, descending into Kitchen Valley, I have distant views south to the mountains of Mexico. Along my return west on Highway 8 toward San Diego, I go north on Viejas Grade. Soon there is a long, sweeping view of the valley below, and cows graze in the meadows. As I proceed north on Viejas Grade, I pass Blessed Virgin Mary Church on the left, with its colorful cemetary, and rock hills silhouetted against a bright blue sky. Ranches along Boulder Creek Road have names like Serenity, Rockin' Chair, Expensive Spread, Fugitive Creek, and Grandpa's Mountains.

I draw a view of Cosmit Peak, which Boulder Creek Road semicircles. It is quiet and peaceful here with a lone, circling hawk and an occasional scurrying squirrel.

"Whale" bus, seen along the back roads

*View of Cosmit Peak, Boulder Creek Road to Julian,
San Diego County*

Back road into Joshua Tree National Park

An unmarked back road near Indio heads up a brown and barren canyon that looks quite forbidding. A sign recommends that I have ample gas, oil, and water. A shacklike ranch has another sign stating that attack dogs are on duty. There are rugged, desert hills all around. Possibly this would have been a bandit hideaway in earlier times. As the canyon narrows, I consider that I wouldn't care to be here if flash flooding were a possibility. The road continues to climb. Joshua trees appear and I cross the National Park boundary. There is a sweeping view of Pleasant Valley dotted with Joshua trees.

Malapai Hill, Joshua Tree National Monument, Riverside County

I sketch the black basalt twin peaks of Malapai Hill and drive on to Squaw Tank. Should you begin this trip from within the park, pick up a brochure at the Squaw Tank turnoff of the main drive. Numbered locations are described in it to help you understand the significant geology to be seen. It may be enough, however, to simply observe the masterful arrangement of boulders (as big as houses) set one upon the other and the rich assortment of desert plants: joshuas, yuccas, needle, and cholla cactus, and many more.

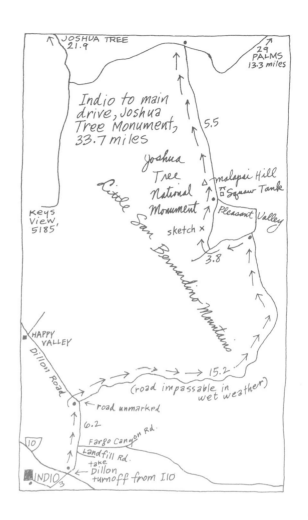

The old ore wagon road to Daggett

Pink desert mountains glow in the distance as I cross a flat desert plain. I'm now traveling on Camp Rock Road, used to haul ore to Lucerne Valley or Daggett in the early days of mining. At dry Anderson Lake motor bikes are scouring up clouds of dust, and at so-called "Rimbender Camp" motor homes are arranged in a circle, like Conestoga wagons of pioneer days. But the desert is vast and all this is forgotten in the appreciation of the purple, chocolate, and salmon-colored splendor of mountains lit by the morning sun. The desert floor is the warm olive hue of a hundred thousand creosote bushes. Coming out of the final canyon pass, I view the Calico Mountains, aptly named because of the many colors painting its peaks and canyons.

View of Ord Mountains from Camp Rock Road on the way to Daggett, San Bernardino County

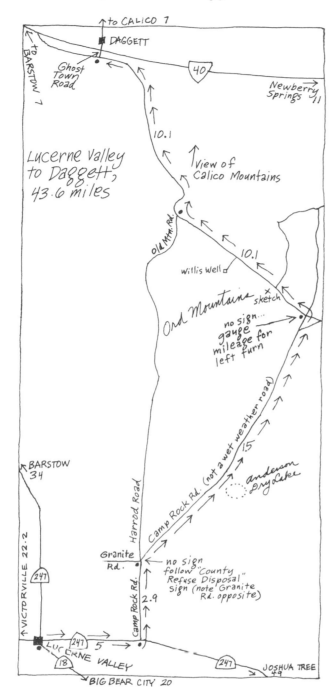

One wagon road to Daggett

to CALICO 7

DAGGETT

to BARSTOW 7

Ghost Town Road

40

Newberry Springs 11

10.1

Lucerne Valley to Daggett, 43.6 miles

View of Calico Mountains

Old Mtn. Rd.

10.1

Willis Well

Ord Mountains   sketch ✕

no sign... gauge mileage for left turn

Camp Rock Rd. (not a wet weather road)

.15

Anderson Dry Lake

BARSTOW 34

Harrod Road

VICTORVILLE 22.2

247

Granite Rd.

Camp Rock Rd.

no sign follow "County Refuse Disposal" sign (note Granite Rd. opposite)

2.9

247

5

Lucerne Valley

18

247   JOSHUA TREE 49

BIG BEAR CITY 20

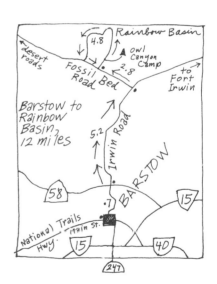

Road to Rainbow Basin

Rainbow Basin

4.8

desert roads

owl Canyon Camp

Fossil Bed Road

2.8

to Fort Irwin

Barstow to Rainbow Basin, 12 miles

5.2

Irwin Road

BARSTOW

58

.7

15

National Trails Hwy.

Main St.

15

247

40

The road to Rainbow Basin

Near Barstow is Rainbow Basin Natural Area. It is a region of uplifted lake beds showing striated and patterned earth. There are variations of purple, beige, chocolate, gray, and green colors in the landscape.

The road winds through Rainbow Basin, giving good opportunities for viewing this unusual area.

Rainbow Basin landscape near Barstow, San Bernardino County

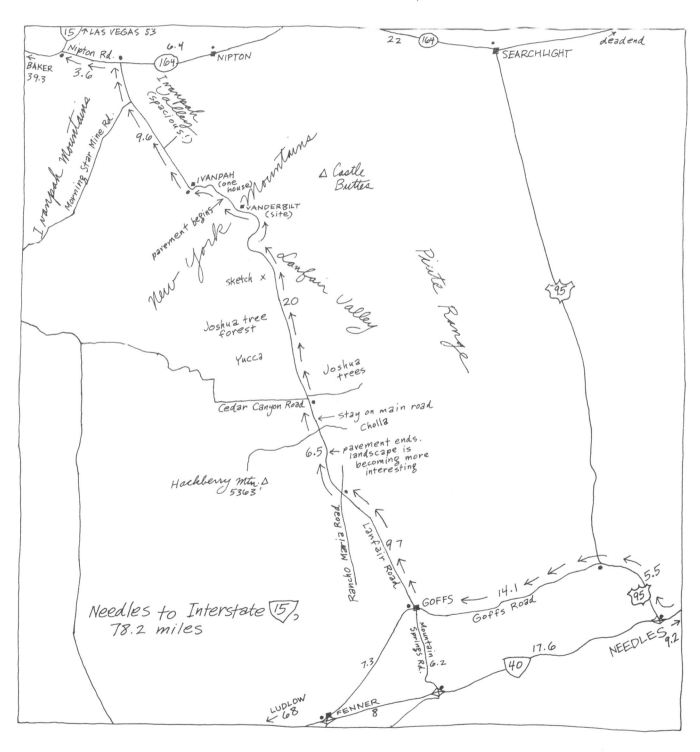

15 ↑LAS VEGAS 53
Nipton Rd. •
6.4
NIPTON
164
22 164
↑deadend
SEARCHLIGHT

BAKER
39.3
3.6

Ivanpah Mountains

Morning Star Mine Rd.

Ivanpah Valley (spacious?)

9.6

IVANPAH (one house)
VANDERBILT (site)

New York Mountains

△ Castle Buttes

Piute Range

pavement begins

95

sketch x

Lanfair Valley

20

Joshua tree forest

Yucca

Joshua trees

Cedar Canyon Road •

stay on main road
Cholla

6.5
pavement ends.
landscape is
becoming more
interesting

Hackberry Mtn. △
5363'

Rancho Maria Road

Lanfair Road
97

GOFFS
14.1
Goffs Road
5.5
95

Needles to Interstate 15,
78.2 miles

Mountain Springs Rd.
6.2

17.6
40

NEEDLES 9.2

7.3

LUDLOW
68
FENNER
8

183

View of the New York Mountains,
Lanfair Valley, San Bernardino
County

The road to Ivanpah (map, page 183)

The desert road becomes more interesting as altitude increases. Mojave yuccas and joshua trees are abundant. There are close views of Piute Range and Castle Mountains across Lanfair Valley.

I sketch the New York Mountains, orange and tan, with mountain juniper dotting them green. The sky just above the peaks is intensely blue. It is quiet here, and I muse how few chances I have to enjoy such profound stillness. When I reach Ivanpah I find but one house near the railroad tracks, with miles and miles of desert silence all around.

Back road to Cima (map, page 186)

I see yuccas and joshuas, forests of them, as I drive toward Cima. Chollas' spiky needles glisten in the sunshine, and range cattle with immense horns sometimes block the road.

The low elevation of the winter sun makes deep shadows in the mountains. I pass through an area forested with juniper, the pinyon pine, then joshua trees again. It is a drive with a rich variety of desert plants to observe.

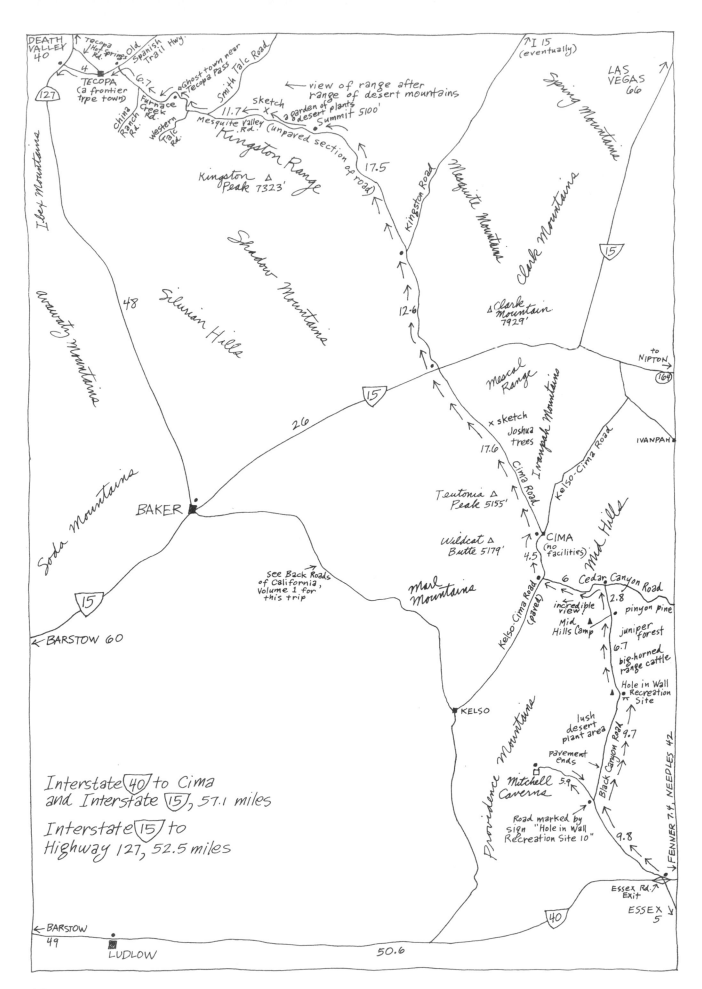

DEATH VALLEY 40

↑ Tecopa
Hot Springs Rd.
Old Spanish Trail Hwy.

127

TECOPA (a frontier type town)

China Ranch Rd.
Furnace Creek Rd.
Western Talc Rd.

6.7

ghost town near Tecopa Pass
Smith Talc Road

11.7

sketch ✕

a garden of desert plants
Summit 5100'

← view of range after range of desert mountains

Mesquite Valley Rd. (unpaved section of road)

Kingston Range

17.5

Kingston Peak 7323' △

Kingston Road

Ibex Mountains

Shadow Mountains

Silurian Hills

48

12.6

Mesquite Mountains

Clark Mountains

Spring Mountains

I 15 (eventually)

LAS VEGAS 66 ↑

15

Clark Mountain 7929' △

to NIPTON

164

Avawatz Mountains

Mescal Range

15

26

Ivanpah Mountains

IVANPAH

✕ sketch Joshua trees

17.6

Cima Road

Kelso-Cima Road

Soda Mountains

BAKER

Teutonia Peak 5155' △

Wildcat Butte 5179' △

CIMA (no facilities)

Mid Hills

15

BARSTOW 60 ←

see Back Roads of California, Volume 1 for this trip

Marl Mountains

4.5

6 Cedar Canyon Road

2.8

Kelso-Cima Road (paved)

incredible view!

Mid Hills Camp

pinyon pine

juniper forest

6.7

big-horned range cattle

Hole in Wall Recreation Site

Providence Mountains

lush desert plant area

Black Canyon Road

9.7

pavement ends

Mitchell Caverns

5.9

FENNER 7.4, NEEDLES 42

KELSO

Road marked by sign "Hole in Wall Recreation Site 10"

9.8

Interstate 40 to Cima and Interstate 15, 57.1 miles

Interstate 15 to Highway 127, 52.5 miles

Essex Rd. Exit

ESSEX 5

40

BARSTOW 49 ←

LUDLOW

50.6

186

Joshua trees
near Cima,
San Bernardino
County

187

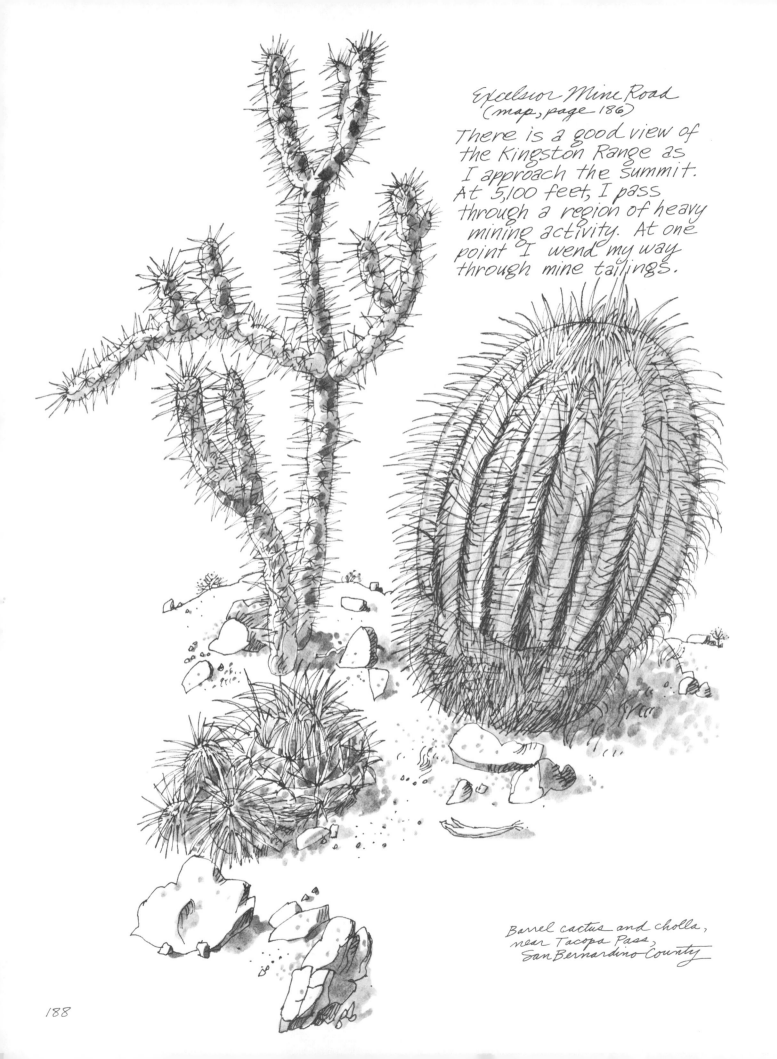

Excelsior Mine Road
(map, page 186)
There is a good view of
the Kingston Range as
I approach the summit.
At 5,100 feet, I pass
through a region of heavy
mining activity. At one
point I wend my way
through mine tailings.

Barrel cactus and cholla,
near Tecopa Pass,
San Bernardino County

I notice garden-like arrangements of cactus and other desert plants growing on the rocky mountainside and choose barrel cactus and cholla to draw.

The road from here descends into a vast desert valley. I pass a ghost town at Tacopa Pass and later pass the frontier-like town of Tacopa before reaching Highway 127.

Epilogue

Picturesque, old-fashioned back roads are in danger of disappearing entirely. They are threatened even in remote and sparsely populated areas of the United States. Like paths, these roads once followed the contours of the land. In fact, many of the roads followed early Indian and pioneer trails.

Today massive machines carve and redistribute the earth to achieve as direct and straight a route as possible. We have all seen road-cuts along our speed-oriented highways. They look to me like ugly wounds that have been inflicted upon the earth. I agree that we must have high-speed freeways and secondary roads; what I object to is the road-building philosophy that _all_ roads are candidates for reconstruction. And from a practical standpoint (as a taxpayer), I am concerned about the increasing costs of road building and maintenance, as more and more widening, cutting, and paving takes place. It is possible that, in many instances, grading the gravel and dirt roads and smoothing the asphalt ones are all that is really necessary.

I don't believe that a straight road is necessarily a safe one. It seems to me that a direct route encourages speed and thus increases the potential for danger.

Arriving at the destination has always been only part of my purpose. It is equally important to me to enjoy the journey itself. (It is _my_ life that is passing by, and I do not wish to waste it peering at freeway asphalt, cars, trucks, and recreational vehicles.)

The price we pay for speed is too high. I feel it is time to slow down, or at least not to increase the pace, especially on back roads.

I have investigated and catalogued back roads in eleven states. My travels have been exhilarating and have given me a great deal of joy. They have left me with a profound concern for the future of the beautiful back roads of America.

Index

Graffiti, Donner Lake Road, Nevada County

Note: Anyone noticing discrepancies in the maps or anyone aware of further changes is encouraged to write to the author at:

19210 Highway 128,
Calistoga, California
94515

Materials used by the author for the making of this book were smooth- or rough-surfaced Fabriano watercolor paper, rapidograph 00 pen with osmiroid ink, bamboo pen with India ink, Winsor & Newton series 233 brushes and Grumbacher 4701 Erminette brushes.

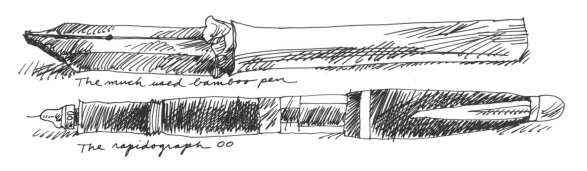

The much used bamboo pen

The rapidograph 00

Historic Spots in California, published by Stanford University Press, was of great help in the author's research.

Book design, drawings, maps, and calligraphy by Earl Thollander